THINKING THINGS THROUGH

Christian reflections on some contemporary ethical issues

Michael Cassidy

ACORN PRESS

Published by Acorn Press Ltd., ABN 50 008 549 540
Office and Orders:
PO Box 282
Brunswick East
Vic 3057
Tel/Fax (03) 9383 1266
International Tel/Fax 61 3 9383 1266
www.acornpress.net.au

National Library of Australia
Cataloguing-in-Publication data
Cassidy, Michael,
 Thinking things through : Christian reflections on some
 contemporary ethical issues.

 ISBN 0 908284 61 6.

 1. Christian ethics. 2. Spiritual direction. I. Title.

241

Printed by Openbook Print, Adelaide
Design and Desk Top Publishing by Communiqué Graphics,
    Mount Waverley
Cover design by Andrew Moody, Blackburn South

Contents

For

Jamie Morrison

Valued friend

assistant extraordinary

and faithful partner in the Gospel

with deep gratitude

PREFACE

Most of the essays which constitute the chapters in this book first appeared as a supplement to the monthly *Update* newsletter of our African Enterprise ministry in South Africa. They seemed to be helpful to many lay people, and indeed to many clergy. Some of them were more strictly focussed in on the theological heart of the Christian faith and these have already appeared in an initial volume entitled *Getting to the Heart of Things – Reflections on Christian Basics*, also published by Acorn Press.

But other essays focussed more into difficult, perplexing and sometimes contentious moral and ethical issues with which the modern church is confronted. So confusing can these issues become that the church in many areas is tempted to succumb to the spirit of the age and allow itself to be seduced into the world's ways of thinking on many of these issues. In fact it is troubling that, in the traffic between the contemporary church and the world, it tends so often to be all one-way, but going in the wrong direction. Instead of challenging the world and its ways, the church risks becoming a spiritual mirror-image of the world and its ways. We are accommodationist rather than prophetic, compromising rather than challenging, and confused rather than clear. We don't lead the world, we follow it. This reflects what one might almost call a loss of nerve amongst many in the church. Add to this the new and fashionable appeals of religious pluralism and syncretism, interfaith rapprochements, plus New Age spirituality and the postmodern anathematising of so-called metanarratives or universal texts, such as the Bible, and we find ourselves facing a crisis amongst many thinking lay people and clergy.

The roll-out and consequences of all of this are many and various. People become hesitant about evangelism and mission. They become confused, withdrawn, and defensive about Judaeo-Christian ethics and morals. They become nervous to step out of line in terms of political correctness and challenge some of the modern postures on sexuality and the biblical nature of marriage and the family. And, of course, in some sectors of the church, there is a temptation even to embrace that perilous contradiction in terms known as "same-sex marriage".

In all of this, truth becomes relativised – likewise morals – and the easy way out is taken of embracing tolerance as the supreme virtue of our time with intolerance made the ultimate sin. In reality, of course, we ought to be socially, legally and religiously tolerant, in the sense of allowing people their views, according them their rights, and loving them regardless of their thought patterns or behaviour. Nevertheless we do not thereby oblige ourselves as Christians to accept the validity of everything under the sun, whether it is true or not, moral or not, historical or not, factual or not, right or wrong. This very easily becomes a perilous capitulation to feeble-mindedness and that can never be the Christian way.

Throughout Jesus' teachings there was a real sense of certain things being right and certain things being wrong, other things being true and yet other things being false. He was not accommodationist in the sense of making way for any kind of behaviour or posture, or any expression of moral or theological views. He was able on occasion to say flatly to the Pharisees: "...you are wrong..." (Mark 12:24a). Then, interestingly enough, He tells them this is because "you know neither the scriptures nor the power of God" (Mark 12:24b). But, in the modern era, if you tell anyone they are wrong about something, you risk being accused immediately of intolerance, superiority, or being neo-this or neo-that, and swearwords start to fly, such as fundamentalist, right-wing, homophobic, bourgeois, or just plain stoopid! The biblical Christian needs lovingly but firmly to reject these postures and stand charitably, firmly and, yes, courageously, on the truth of the New Testament in terms of its postures on theology, spirituality, the way of salvation, ethics, morality, family life, marriage, sexuality, social responsibility, and so on.

So it was out of concerns about all this that these essays were born. They are modest in scope, especially considering the enormity of some of the issues addressed. But many people do not have the time to read vast tomes on these matters and only need a manageable statement setting out the headlines of the issue in a manner both comprehensible and reflective of a genuine attempt to be faithful to the Christian Scriptures. I must also acknowledge right up front that these thoughts come from an amateur. I am a layperson, not a professional theologian or ethicist. Even so, I have felt constrained like many laypeople to struggle with these things, and my modest thoughts are hereby offered. If the professionals see superficiality, I hope at least that ordinary fellow strugglers will find some clarity and be helped along the way.

For some, these essays will often suffice and, for others, they may at least pave the way to taking the matter further with other reading. If this should happen with readers of this present volume, I will feel happily rewarded. My end notes to each chapter may suggest further reading for those seeking to dig deeper.

Just as with *Getting to the Heart of Things*, I want to thank our African Enterprise colleagues in Australia, and especially Mike Woodall and David Hewetson, who motivated this venture. David also helped ably and judiciously in the editing of some of the essays. Significant research and editing help was also forthcoming from my writing and publishing assistant, Jamie Morrison, whose labours on this volume and on its end notes have been herculean. Likewise much appreciation to former American intern Steve Offutt and to Jonathan Wilson, formerly in our AE Pan African Leadership Training ministries, now taking up a leadership role in another ministry in Canada. Legal specialist Kristen Romens was a huge help with the chapter on capital punishment. Thanks are also due to various other friends for their help in reading certain chapters and offering valuable insights and suggestions. In this regard, I am grateful to Dieter Achtzehn, Richard Bewes, Mark Kumleben, Dereck Stone and, once again, to David Hewetson. Extensive typing endeavours were also put in by Heather Valentine, formerly in our office in Sydney, and by my former secretary, Colleen Smith, here in South Africa, as well as by my present secretary, Brenda

Harrison. Thanks go to Andrea Benn, also in our Sydney office, for all her help in shuttling the manuscript between us in South Africa and Acorn Press. My deep thanks go also to Gill Dobson, my personal assistant, who held down the correspondence fort while I completed work on the manuscript. I extend also special appreciation to Bishop John Wilson and Rena Pritchard at Acorn Press. They did a beautiful job of publishing the first volume and this one now follows in that same tradition.

As always, I must thank my precious wife, Carol, who makes space for me to work hard in my various endeavours for the Lord, even when sometimes she pays a sacrificial price in terms of my time spent in writing and other things. She is a star – no, a supernova!

Finally, I want to dedicate this volume to Jamie Morrison, who has not only helped me hugely with this volume, but who has for many years been not only a faithful and industrious assistant and a deeply valued partner in the Gospel, but a treasured friend with whom I have shared joy, pain, tears, laughter, valleys, mountaintops and thousands of hours of extended work and labours for the Lord. Without his help, I would not have managed the nine years we have worked together so far. Thank you, Jamie, so much. You are very special to me.

Now may the Lord bless and find ways to use the modest offering of these pages.

Michael Cassidy
Pietermaritzburg, South Africa

Chapter One

ETHICS

I want in this opening chapter to try to build a fundamental understanding of how a Christian should, in general terms, approach ethics. I describe this approach as finding the "Jesus way" of living in all areas of life and behaviour, not only personal and marital, but also social, political and economic.

In a nutshell, my thesis is that the biblical ethic is one which is built into the moral fabric of the universe by Jesus himself as the agent of creation: "...all things were made through him, and without him was not anything made that was made" (John 1:3). As people are led to understand this and as they see the Christian ethic as the friend and not the enemy of their joy and fulfilment, they can arrive at a sure and stable moral foundation for their lives.

Contradictions and confusions

To start with, let's recognise that many different and intriguing views are propounded in the area of ethics. Some say: "What is moral is what you feel good after." Others see morals as a blind obedience to someone's arbitrary words of command. The religious prude might put it this way: "If it's fun, it must be wrong." Postmodernism makes all ethics relative – there are no absolutes. Broadmindedness towards everything is the order of the day, and tolerance the final virtue. Some feel that what the majority in a political party, or the majority in a society decrees becomes right as an ethical norm. Precarious indeed.

All this shows that morality is a confusing subject surrounded by multitudes of views. In trying to find the correct one, I would like to think that we are embarking on an inquiry into the true and the good; and that everyone is genuinely participating in this quest, even perhaps those who deny the possibility of truth and goodness. After all, they still want to find the best and happiest way to live!

What, then, is truth?

As I understand it, truth is the properly construed meaning of all experience. It is a judgement or proposition which, when followed out into the total witness of all the facts in our experience, does not disappoint our expectations. For example, if I say there are five pies in the kitchen for you and you go there and do in fact find five pies, then the facts of your experience do not disappoint the expectation raised by my statement. In other words, your experience confirms my statement as true.

Or we could say that truth is a judgement which corresponds to things as they are. It is a statement which accords with reality on a 1:1 ratio. Thus if I hold up a watch and say, "This is a knife", then the statement is untrue because it does not accord with reality on a 1:1 ratio. But if I say, "This is a watch", the statement is true because it does accord with reality on a 1:1 ratio.

So, if I, as a Christian, say: "Jesus died on the Cross and was alive three days later and is Lord of heaven and earth", I believe I am making a true statement because I believe it accords with reality and with facts as they are on a 1:1 ratio. When the Muslim says Jesus did not die on the Cross and was not raised the third day but simply ascended into heaven, we have an issue of truth and historical fact before us. And the law of antithesis – A is not non-A – dictates that two contradictory factual statements cannot both be true at the same time.

Truth's validity

With the law of antithesis clearly in our minds, we must note that truth's validity is also determined by its ability to make sense out of life. Thus, when we look at the human being we find him or her to be religious – "incurably religious" said Marx – but also rational and moral. A true statement, therefore, will be one which makes sense out of that fact, or any other relevant data bearing upon that fact. What cause explains that kind of effect, i.e., how and why are we creatures who are religious, rational and moral? What is the *true* explanation of this?

Moral truth, therefore, will be that understanding of morality which is in accordance with the facts and realities of moral experience. And even if arriving at this understanding is not easy, we will nevertheless follow – if we are pursuing the issue with integrity – that understanding of morality which has the fewest difficulties and inconsistencies. We will not simply retreat into darkness as we see light or give up the search for truth just because it is demanding or complicated.

Christian morality

I believe that traditional Christian morality is in accordance with the facts and realities of moral experience. Such morality is in contrast to the secular, post-Christian age which, in its marginalisation of God, has pulled the very foundation out from under any real system of ethics. That is, if God is dead then there is no real or absolute basis for morality. The great tradition of Christian theology which runs from Augustine to Thomas Aquinas has always affirmed that there is a moral law bearing its own evidence and authority and that humans can apprehend the reality and existence of this moral inheritance. Said the Apostle Paul: "...what the law requires is written on their hearts" (Romans 2:15a). Naturally, therefore, Christians do not believe that human life, love and moral experience can be understood or even described adequately except in relation to that which transcends them, and that transcendent factor is what Christians call God.

This leads us to the threefold basis of Christian morality which shows that Christian morality is not freedom from rules, but freedom *with* rules – or freedom *within* rules. This requires us to look at:
- The nature of human beings
- The nature of the universe
- The nature of God as revealed in Jesus Christ

The nature of human beings

Who are we? First of all, we note that we exist! Self-evident of course, but it is important to state that we are here as against not being here! That is a mystery in itself. And the most important things about us as human beings are not quantitative, but qualitative – i.e., our interior life and experience as spirit beings. What matters most to us is not mass, velocity, electrons, or our chemical make-up, but value, purpose, love, friendship, service, beauty, goodness, mutual care, and so on.

Beyond that, we apprehend reality and can make sense of it. We are rational creatures and, when we deeply study reality we feel, or at least most do, that mind (ours) is meeting Mind (God's). The things we study and apprehend are not nonsensical. We can make sense of them and we ourselves are not putting truth anywhere; we are just uncovering or discovering truth which is already there, regardless of the field of study we are thinking about.

Is morality just social conditioning?

Some people will say that all morals are variable and different between one society and another. However, most sociologists and anthropologists would, I believe, agree with C.S. Lewis, who said that, while differences do exist in the moralities of different nations, these differences are not total.[1] We cannot imagine a country where people were admired for cowardice, deception, theft, cruelty, selfishness or incest. People "have differed as to whether you should have one wife or four. But they have always agreed that you must not simply have any woman you liked."[2] Further, the fact that we can think of the morality of one group being better or worse than that of another is to introduce a value judgement beyond them both and reflect an ultimate standard. "A man does not call a line crooked unless he has some idea of a straight line", said Lewis.[3]

Lewis speaks of two key points for us to register: "First, that human beings, all over the earth, have this curious idea that they ought to behave in a certain way, and cannot really get rid of it. Secondly, that they do not in fact behave in that way. They know the Law of Nature; they break it. These two facts are the foundation of all clear thinking about ourselves and the universe we live in."[4]

Is there anything behind the law?

The question now presents itself as to whether there is anything behind the Law as we see it in Scripture and in our hearts. Christians answer this question in the affirmative, and believe that this sense of something behind reality is, in fact, revealed in Jesus as the *Logos*, or Self-expression of God, who has stepped onto our planet to bring the explanation we need as to origins, life, morality and ultimate destiny.

We need now to look at the second basis of morality, namely the nature of the universe.

The nature of the universe

The big question

The big question is, do we really live in a universe? Is reality really turned (Latin: *versus*) into one (Latin: *unus*)? Or do we believe that we live in a "multiverse", a random, chaotic, unrelated, unpredictable and irregular order of reality? The Christian understands the term "universe" as a genuinely theological word. It speaks about a reality which is turned into one or which coheres in unity through a unifying principle. Christians believe that there is indeed a unity in the universe – hence its name – and that there is an internal cohesion. This is brought about by the infinite-personal God who exists and who, in an orderly fashion, made things together in relationships and in harmony. In fact, if our original cause is physical and accidental, there is no explanation for mind or spirit or design. The effect is not explained by such a cause. But starting from mind, all becomes explicable, not just in the physical and material universe, but humans within it, along with the moral sense humans manifest.

God-given laws

That being so, the Christian who takes the Bible's view of reality seriously believes that in every area of life – including the moral – there are indeed God-given laws built into the very fabric of the cosmic reality around us. God has spoken both in nature and in the Bible and the whole created order belongs to him. The God of nature is also the God of grace. Thus the laws of Scripture and the laws of nature have the same law-giver. Even the ancients, without the Bible, could see this. So Cicero could write:

> There is indeed a true law – right reason – that is in harmony with Nature and present in all things, unchanging and eternal and

that guides us to our duty by its commands and deflects us from wrongdoing by its prohibitions. Its commands and prohibitions never fail to prevail with the good but they have no power to influence the wicked. It is not right (*fas*) to legislate against the requirements of this law and it is not permitted to limit its application. It is impossible for it to be repealed in its entirety and we cannot be exempted from this law even by the Roman people or by the Senate. We do not need to seek out an Sextus Aelius to interpret or expound this law nor will there be one law in Rome, another in Athens, one law at one time and a different one some time later. One eternal and unchanging law will govern all peoples at all times and it will be, as it were, the single ruling and commanding god of the whole human race. That god is the creator of the law, its proclaimer and its enforcer. The man who does not obey this law is denying his own nature and, by rejecting his human nature, he will incur the greatest of punishments, even though he will have evaded the other things that are thought of as penalties."[5]

Thus could professor (and Bishop) F.R. Barry, a noted British ethicist of yesteryear, observe that, likewise for Aristotle, the great Greek philosopher (384–322 BC), morality is "an aspect of the whole cosmic 'movement' or process, rooted in the structure of the universe, and is, indeed, conformity with that movement – the nature of things – on the part of man."[6]

Speaking about developed Stoicism – the philosophical school of thought founded about 308BC by Zeno and teaching that virtue was the highest good[7] – Barry notes that "The Stoics taught that all men partake in the divine reason, informing and ruling the Cosmos. (They never, however, made up their minds whether the universe was 'one big machine' or 'one big soul' [*anima mundi*]…)".[8]

In any event, says Barry, "Through this reason, controlling the passions, men could discern the true laws of life – the moral law – implanted by nature in the human mind, capable of rational demonstration, and binding at all times on all men. Thus virtue, the fulfilment of man's being, is found to consist in 'following nature', that is, obeying the natural law."[9]

My point here is that the idea of "natural law" which has been so much at the heart of Christian ethical thinking from the start, did not in itself originate in a Christian philosophical framework. It first began to be articulated in Greek philosophy, was then elaborated on by Roman writers, then worked into the ethical systems of the Stoics, and later taken over by the Christian church and made foundational to Christian moral philosophy over the centuries. So, for example, Thomas Aquinas could insist that what is right, and what really *ought to be done* by humans, is ultimately grounded not in some arbitrary decree but in what *is*, and what exists as part of the very nature of the universe around us.

It has been pointed out that, when the Greeks first began to explore the nature of reality and the world, they were fascinated by the great variety of customs (*mores*) and the social and moral laws which they encountered all around them. But they also noted that some of these laws and customs seemed to be common to all peoples everywhere. These they concluded must be there by nature (Greek: *phusei*), having been implanted by nature itself into the lives and consciences of humankind, with such laws being prior to and therefore more authoritative than the various laws coming to us by social convention.

Thus it was that the Apostle Paul could later say, rather as a Stoic might, that "When Gentiles who have not the law do by nature what the law requires, they are a law to themselves, even though they do not have the law. They show that what the law requires is written on their hearts, while their conscience also bears witness and their conflicting thoughts accuse or perhaps excuse them..." (Romans 2:14-15).

Likewise we register Paul's profound condemnation of homosexual or same-sex sexual relationships as being "contrary to nature" and against the natural order of things, i.e., unnatural (Greek: *para phusin* i.e., "against nature"), and therefore immoral and wrong from a Christian perspective. His point here is that the morality of such acts is not determined by an arbitrary decree of humans, but by laws which are inherent in nature and which are contravened by such behaviour.

As the Christian church entered the Roman Empire, and found this kind of moral thinking prevalent, so, not surprisingly, Christian thinkers took this over. The fact is that this idea of a universal reasoning and morality informing and enlightening all humankind seemed to fit in with the *Logos* doctrine and John's belief and teaching about "The true light that enlightens every man..." (John 1:9).

And so to that *Logos* doctrine we turn.

The *Logos*

The Greeks had said that this Divine Reason, which rules the cosmos, which gives it coherence, unity and order, and which is the basis of the inherent morality we are aware of, does have a name and they called it the *Logos*. This meant the "Word" or "self-expression" of God. John the Apostle knew this and tied it to Jesus whom he identified as the "Logos made flesh". Thus he used the Greeks' own word for the great unifying and coherent principle at the heart of all reality when he wrote the prologue to his gospel, saying: "In the beginning was the Logos, and the Logos was with God, and the Logos was God... And the *Logos became flesh* and dwelt among us, full of grace and truth; we have beheld his glory, glory as of the only Son from the Father" (John 1:1,14). For John, Jesus is this unifying, coherent principle. In other words, this principle is more than a principle; it is a person – Jesus himself, for "in him all things hold together" (Colossians 1:17).

Notes Barry: "Christian teachers early began to claim that the God of the Bible was himself the Author of the law of nature, which had been expressed for Israel in the Decalogue and was indeed reaffirmed by the Lord himself. 'So far from despising the best moral teaching given by Jew or pagan in their age, both [St. Paul and St. Peter] endorse it, while at the same time giving it deeper foundations and more far-reaching scope.' In Christ the true way of life had been personified – this *is* life according to nature. Seen in those terms, it has been suggested, Christians can regard the natural law doctrine (in its Christian or 'catholic' form) as a declaration of the Lordship of Christ over all human life."[10]

Barry continues: "Eventually the classical Christian statement was formulated, as everyone knows, by St Thomas who, by an amazing *tour de force* brought together the Stoic law of nature, Aristotle, Cicero and the Bible and the content of Christian revelation in one magnificent, all-containing synthesis, which may be called the charter of Christendom and indeed supplied the intellectual basis for a universal Christian civilisation. The natural law doctrine, thus formulated, survived the upheaval of the Reformation and is still the officially recognised basis of Roman Catholic moral theology. On the reformed side of the watershed, both Luther and Calvin use it in their own ways."[11]

Interestingly enough, the great Anglican Archbishop, William Temple, one of my favourite writers on natural theology, used this line to great effect in his book *Nature, Man and God*.[12]

All this brings us to a readiness to look at the distinctively Christian pillar of the nature of God, which we now add to the other two pillars of morality, namely the nature of humanity and the nature of the universe.

The nature of God

Christians believe that what Jesus was, as seen in his earthly life and ministry, God is always. Jesus' nature is God's nature. Not only that, but in his humanity he was the natural, normal man *par excellence*, whose life was in absolute accord with the natural and divine order of the cosmos, which he had himself made. No wonder He could affirm, "All authority in heaven and on earth has been given to me" (Matthew 28:18b).

The point is that, for Christians, Jesus is not just a great religious prophet and the finest man who ever lived. He in fact is either much more or much less. The New Testament obviously says He is much more. He is the Cosmic Christ who is the creator of the whole universe and the one behind it. The New Testament goes on to assert that, while God the Father was the author of the creation idea, Jesus the Son was the agent in the whole creating process. In the prologue of John's gospel, John says: "...all things were made through him, and without him was not anything made that was made" (John 1:3).

The Apostle Paul for his part could affirm that: "...all things were created through him and for him. He is before all things, and in him all things hold together" (Colossians 1:16b-17).

A similar line comes from the writer to the Hebrews and he is very succinct and clear about this Cosmic Christ when he writes that He "bears the very stamp of his [God's] nature, upholding the universe by his word of power" (Hebrews 1:3). Jesus was not just a rather unusual Middle Eastern preacher or prophet or teacher, trotting out here and there a few bits of pretty religious advice. Rather He is the creator, Lord, upholder and sustainer of the entire universe. Yes, indeed all authority and power in the cosmos and on earth have indeed been given to Him, as we noted a moment ago in Matthew 28:18.

If this is the case, and Jesus is the one behind the universe, then it is His stamp which is on and written into the very fabric of the universe. And it's exactly for this reason that we have to tell society, both governments and governed, and ordinary individuals, that if life is to work satisfactorily, whether it relates to matters that are private or social, economic or political, marital or sexual, then the game must be played Jesus' way. Otherwise it simply will not work.

Morality as exposed and not imposed

What Christians believe, then, is that Jesus did not impose an artificial morality on human beings but only exposed more fully the intrinsic morality which was already there and which He had stamped into the universe as the way things were meant to function. A moral action, therefore, will not only have Jesus and Scripture behind it, but the universe and the cosmos. A bad or evil action by contrast will not only stand under the judgement of God and Scripture, but under the judgement of life and the cosmos.

Christian ethics are, therefore, always on the side of fullness, happiness, true fun, completeness, peace, health, sexual and romantic fulfilment, plus psychological wholeness, mental health and spiritual joy. And indeed social stability.

In the bad old days of apartheid in South Africa, I wrote a book which sought to address the issue of socio-political morality and I was seeking to make the point that apartheid flew in the face of an intrinsic morality stamped in the universe and therefore would never work. In fact, I wrote to one of the senior politicians in the apartheid cabinet and said that, in my view, the real issue before the apartheid government was whether we lived in a moral universe or not. If we did not, then they could carry on with apartheid and might ultimately get away with it. But if we lived in a moral universe as made by Jesus Christ, and if we were going against the Jesus way, then the discriminatory policies of apartheid with their undermining of human dignity would ultimately bring about the disintegration of the society and its implosion in a cataclysm of racial fury and social rage.

In seeking at that time to make my point about morality as exposed rather than imposed, I wrote this:

> What this means is that in all phases of life in the universe there is "the way" and "not-the-way". In chemistry H2O produces water. We may fight the formula or twist it into something else, but in the end we have to surrender to it and accept it or we won't get water. Two parts of hydrogen and one of oxygen is the way, and everything else, for example H3O, is not-the-way.

> Likewise, when I fly from Durban to Johannesburg, there is a way to fly and there is not-the-way. Check with the pilot and he will tell you that every moment he must obey those laws upon which flying depends – or else! There can be no moral holidays in the air. He obeys or breaks. And he gains mastery only by obedience. Aviation did not invent those laws or impose them; it discovered them.

> Now if obedience to laws holds good in the physical realm, what about when we come to the business of human living and when we move over into more subtle relationships like the social, the moral, the spiritual or the political? Does chance reign there? Can we do as we please and get away with it? Or do we find there something which demands obedience if we are to live happily and in peace? And is that something which demands our co-operation not merely a set of conventions and customs built up by society but something written into the nature of reality? The philosopher Immanuel Kant (1724–1804) once said, "Two things strike me with awe: the starry heavens above and the moral law within." What he meant was that the laws of those two worlds are equally dependable, equally authoritative, and equally inescapable. And there is a way and "not-the-way" written into both. If we obey the way, we get results. If we don't we get consequences, dreadful consequences.

> In other words, we accommodate our lives, bodies and functions to the laws of the universe as we know them. It also follows that if God is behind everything, then human beings should fit into the environment which is there. And this is indeed the case, for example, in the physical realm.

> So for the Christian it is not surprising that my lung system is in correlation to the world's atmosphere, for the same reasonable God made both my lung system and the atmosphere, and he put me in this world. He gave me an eye which registers colour and a world which is colourful. He gave me an ear to hear sounds and a world full of sound.
>
> In short, the Christian believes that in every area and realm of life there are God-given laws built into the fabric of reality. God has spoken both in nature and in the Bible, and the whole created order belongs to Him.[13]

That being the case, we have to play the game of life His way. Coming back to Aquinas for a moment, we can register with theologian Richard Niebuhr that: "Underlying the synthesis of Aquinas is the resolution to discover the basis of right in the given, created nature of man and his world. His insistence that the ought is founded on the is ... depends on the Christian belief that the Creator and Saviour are one."[14]

This is the really key thing people need to understand. Life which is not lived in the Jesus way is not finally in their own interests, nor does it bring true happiness and fulfilment because it requires living at odds with the moral fabric of the "Jesus-created" universe around us.

In a sense, what all of this puts before us is the very serious question as to whether contemporary postmodernist thinkers are right in the notion of every person being the creator of their own values, morals, behavioural norms, belief systems etc. Or whether there is not indeed an objective right and wrong which is morally authoritative for all people at all times and in all ages, and that it is there prior to all man-made systems of morality and ethical behaviour.

If it is really a matter of each society or individual simply deciding what is right or wrong for them, or morally acceptable or unacceptable in terms of behaviour, then all the Greek and Roman thinkers going right back to antiquity and all Christian moral theologians over the last two thousand years stand in error and self-deception.

But if the latter are right, and if there is a certain "naturalness" to morals, then we find ourselves stumbling or tumbling into the true heart of ethics and morality.

Morality as cooperation with the cosmos

This means that morality, from the Christian point of view, is a cooperation with the cosmic reality and the moral environment which is around us. To disregard that reality or that environment is therefore to put oneself in peril. To be moral, therefore, for the Christian is not to be narrow and prudish but simply to cooperate with the moral and spiritual structure of reality.

So the moral law is the law of nature and the law of nature is the law of life. Thus the laws of God's world all interlock so that, when humans are called to be moral, they are simply being called to play the game of life according to the rules of the game established by the author of the game for our happiness and well-being.

Coming back to F.R. Barry, he puts it this way:

> We are creatures: "he [God] made us and not we ourselves." If we are to continue to live at all we must accept certain conditions inherent in the way the world works. If we try to exploit the soil we die of starvation... Nature is only controlled by obeying her. As man through obedience learns more about the regularities of nature – the "laws" of nature, built-in to the structure – it becomes to him an intelligible order with which he is able increasingly to co-operate, to bring more of its elements under conscious control and to find enlarging possibilities of freedom and fulfilment in living. Obedience is the way of freedom and self-realisation – obedience, not to an arbitrary decree but to the way things are, the structure of life. But if we try to defy that we destroy ourselves. God is not mocked. There is a law of consequences. "Things are what they are and the consequences will be what they will be."[15]

Barry adds:

> But the physical environment is not all. Men are related not only to nature but to other persons and to their societies. (There is no evidence of pre-social man). There are moral as well as physical conditions, and these too are built-in to the structure of the universe. Here too man has to discover and learn to obey certain principles or laws which are inherent in and govern interpersonal relationships and any workable form of social order. The moral law is part of the way the world is made. What is "good" is that which enhances life by obedience to its inherent constitution, what is "bad" is what is out of relation to the structure of the world and life as it is – theists, of course, will say, to the will of God...

The moral law is the law of nature and the law of nature is the way of life. The whole experience of the human race corroborates that there are certain principles which lead to full and successful living both for individuals and for societies, others which lead to breakdown or dissolution. In the moral order no less than in the physical there is inevitably a law of consequences. God is not mocked. The wages of sin is death. If men ignore or defy the natural law they will destroy themselves and their societies: and that, after all, was the message of the Prophets.[16]

Salvation as harmony

So when Christians call on people to find salvation in Christ, they are in fact calling them to an all-embracing harmony in which their divided souls and bodies can be unified in right relationships with the world, with other personal centres of consciousness, with the infinite spiritual environment, and with God himself in Christ.

Christians, therefore, believe that, in Christ, the end and meaning of human life and the universe are revealed. In Him is the basic structure of morality. For a person to come to Christ is thus the way to become genuinely human. It is the way of fulfilment. The late Bishop Stephen Neill wrote a book called *A Genuinely Human Existence*.[17] In it, he said that to come to Christ is to take the first really great step to becoming genuinely human.

Conversion is vital

Given all we have said above, it will be obvious why biblical Christians see conversion as so vital. You see, in Christian conversion an extraordinary thing happens. Even though you and I fail to keep God's laws and standards, and experience unhappy consequences as a result, nevertheless we approve of the Law more and more and want to keep it once we have come to Christian conversion.

Being in a love relationship with Christ, we not only want to obey him for our own selfish well-being, but because we love him and want to please him. It is this which brings the glorious element of freedom into Christian obedience. So our liturgies speak of one "whose service is perfect freedom".[18]

As for the Christian's moral relationships with others, they are to be controlled by the ethic of Christian love. Said Jesus: "...love one another, as I have loved you" (John 15:12). And the love he had for us was absolute, final, inexhaustible, sacrificial – and it issued in service and servanthood. It is on that love, finally, that Christian morality stands.

Conclusion

This is why I feel so strongly that wherever we as Christians are called to serve and flourish we should not abandon either Christian faith and commitment or biblical values, ethics and absolutes as we see them in the Christian Scriptures, namely the Bible. Because for me what we see in the Bible, and most specifically in Jesus and his words, is not just one in a pantheon of religious options. Rather do we see here a description and explanation of the *way things are* in the universe and in life. This being so, there is only one way to play the game of life if it is really to work, and that is the Jesus way, because this is Jesus' universe and he is the Author of it and the one behind it. Says the writer to the Hebrews: He upholds "the universe by His word of power" (Hebrews 1:3). That is why He could also say, "I am the way..." (John 14:6). This was not just the Way to the Father – but the Way for everything in terms of life and behaviour.

If a person can find Christ as Saviour, Lord and Friend, then he or she has truly found the pathway to peace, the highway to happiness, the secret of service and the personal key to Christian ethics. And can any experience be more magnificent than that?

End Notes

1. C.S. Lewis, *Mere Christianity* (New York: Macmillan, 1977), 19-21.

2. Lewis, 19.

3. Lewis, 45.

4. Lewis, 21.

5. Niall McCloskey, *Cicero*, University of Saskatchewan, Department of Classics, Classics 233.3(01), Introduction to Ancient Thought, 2004, <http://duke.usask.ca/~niallm/233/Cicero.htm> (March 2, 2006).

6. F.R. Barry, *Christian Ethics and Secular Society* (London: Hodder & Stoughton, 1966), 41.

7. Stoicism is a school of philosophy founded (308 BC) in Athens by Zeno of Citium (Cyprus). It teaches self-control and detachment from distracting emotions, sometimes interpreted as an indifference to pleasure or pain. This allows one to be a clear thinker, level-headed and unbiased. In practice, Stoicism is intended to imbue an individual with virtue, wisdom, and integrity of character. Students are encouraged to help those in need, knowing that those who can, should. Stoicism also teaches psychological independence from society, regarding it as an unruly and often unreasonable entity while encouraging active engagement in improving society. Later Stoic writers were Seneca, Epictetus and Marcus Aurelius. (Definition of Stoicism taken from Stoicism, 1 March 2006, Wikipedia, <http://en.wikipedia.org/wiki/Stoicism>, 2 March 2006.)

8. Barry, 42.

9. Barry, 42.

10. Barry 42; italics his.

11. Barry 42-43.

12. William Temple, *Nature, Man and God* (New York: Macmillan, 1964).

13. Michael Cassidy, *The Passing Summer* (London: Hodder & Stoughton, 1989), 216-217.

14. Richard Niebuhr, *Christ and Culture* (London: Faber & Faber, 1952), 148.

15. Barry, 48-49.

16. Barry 49-50.

17. Stephen Neill, *A Genuinely Human Existence* (Garden City, New York: Doubleday & Co., 1959).

18. From 'A Collect for Peace', Anglican *Book of Common Prayer*.

Chapter Two

THE MORALS, ETHICS AND PRINCIPLES OF CHRISTIAN MARRIAGE

In our last chapter we reflected on ethics generally and in very broad terms sought to establish that there is a Jesus way of living maximally and fulfillingly in this world. The Jesus way is based on the idea that the biblical ethic is built into the moral fabric of the universe by Jesus himself as the agent of creation. I want now, and in these coming chapters, to look at specific areas of life which involve ethical decisions and see how we can apply the Jesus way to them. I begin with Christian marriage, the home and family life.

Growing confusion

The issues of marriage and family life were once relatively easy to address. But now confusion reigns as to the nature of the family, what constitutes a family, whether it is necessary to get married, how to stay married if you do get married, on what basis you can get out of marriage, and whether two gays or lesbians can or should marry according to the normal rites of the Church (see chapter six). Such confusion in the adult community leads, of course, to rampant and full-blown confusion amongst young people.

Actually this whole controversy about marriage and sexuality is interrelated with the much larger debate going on today about God and Jesus, the Bible, hermeneutics (the science of interpretation), nature, the future, and even life beyond the grave. However, American writer James Davison Hunter, author of *Culture Wars*, describes the situation with these words, "In the final analysis there may be much more to the contemporary culture war than the struggle for the family, yet there is little doubt that the issues contested in the realm of family life are central to the larger struggle and are perhaps fateful for other battles being waged."[1] In short, the ethics we embrace in the area of marriage and issues surrounding marriage have a tremendous impact on all other areas of life.

Unfortunately, it is a discouraging time for the institution of marriage.

"A crumbling institution"

In an instructive and insightful article in the September 2004 edition of *Christianity Today* magazine, David Gushee, professor of moral philosophy at Union University in Jackson, Tennessee, speaks about Christian marriage in the United States as "a crumbling institution." He talks about how social revolutions have cracked the pillars of marriage and dramatically weakened this sacred institution. Indeed, he sees marriage in a "stunning state of fragility" and he lists a number of different types of revolution which have played into this. These revolutions he lists[2] as follows:

The sexual revolution

In the 1960s a liberal view of sex began to say that sexual intercourse should be confined to "loving relationships", or else whenever desired, provided there was mutual consent. Thus did sex begin to get separated from marriage.

The contraception and abortion revolutions

Both of these helped to jump-start the sexual revolution and, in 1972 the U.S. Supreme Court allowed states to extend access to contraceptives as and when required by the unmarried. In 1973 there was the *Roe vs. Wade* decision relating to abortion and this resulted in a mighty rush on abortions resulting back then in one out of three U.S. pregnancies ending in elective abortion, but finally settling down to one in four or five today. This has resulted in more than a million developing children per year being killed in America. In the *Roe vs. Wade* Supreme Court decision, the rights and interests of children were diminished over against those of adults. In other words, "The interests of children must give way to the interests of adults."

The illegitimacy revolution

With about 33 percent of all children in America being born to unwed mothers, the spirit of acceptance for illegitimate children began to carry the day and even the notion of illegitimacy began to be seen as insensitive or oppressive. Gushee writes: "If one of marriage's key purposes had been to provide a framework of family relations for a child's world, then the illegitimacy revolution marked the crumbling of this pillar."

The cohabitation revolution

The other revolutions just mentioned began to produce this one so that in the U.S. at this time some four million unmarried couples live together, many of them doing this "as a trial run for matrimony." Researchers, however, point out that cohabitation as a trial run for marriage does not prepare couples well for that commitment and a high percentage of cohabiting couples who do finally get married also finally end up in divorce. It's like testing a parachute with a ten-foot jump. It's just not long enough. Those in trial-run "marriages" also suffer much higher levels of "conflict, domestic violence, abuse, and infidelity than married partners do." Research also reveals that, in cohabiting contexts, there is a much greater likelihood of abuse of children. These relationships, incidentally, last on average only five years.

The reproduction revolution

Ever since the first test tube baby was produced in Britain in 1978, assisted reproduction techniques have developed and proliferated and have, not surprisingly, attracted many thousands of couples eager and hopeful to have children. While at one level this has been a blessing to numbers of married couples, nevertheless it has also made assisted reproduction (AR) possible for all kinds of combinations of people willing to pay for it – for example, two men, or two women, or an unmarried couple, or a single woman or man. Or even two men and one woman and so on. This latter phenomenon has further weakened the link between marriage and parenting.

The divorce revolution

Prior to the 1960s, divorce was an exit mechanism from marriage which was very much a last resort. And although in secular society about one in four marriages ended in divorce, only approximately one in forty marriages among committed

Christians ended in divorce. But all that has dramatically changed, divorce has become exceedingly common, even among Christians, and of course along with that the rise of the related phenomenon of remarriage as well as what some people call "serial monogamy". This means having a series of spouses, one after the other.

Gushee notes that "statistically, remarriages and especially cohabitation relationships are even less enduring than first marriages, further multiplying cases of serial monogamy."

The gay rights revolution

Although we will come to this in chapter six, we mention here the seventh revolution which is the gay rights revolution. Gushee notes that "the damage homosexuality does to marriage takes two forms. First, promiscuous gay sex represents yet another demolished boundary (gender) in this sexual revolution. Second, the move on the part of many in the gay community to press for full civil equality for their relationships, even 'marriage', assaults the very definition of the institution. And just think of the further escalating complications once gay couples start adopting children."

* * * * * *

Clearly then, all of these different revolutions have placed the marriage institution as traditionally understood at a very difficult, precarious and complex place. However, let's make no mistake. All this is also perilous in the extreme in terms of the social consequences for men, women and children when this most basic of divine institutions is placed in jeopardy.

Nevertheless, with all that said, we must not and dare not, as Christians, give up on the Bible's view of marriage and family life. As we continue to live in our tumultuous and confusing present-day culture and at the same time struggle to establish within our own homes the Jesus way for marriage, there are some positive steps we can take which will allow us to pattern our relationships on God's original intentions.

In thinking of these biblical steps we can liken them to procedures taken from the instruction book which comes with a new camera, or CD player, or motorcar. The manufacturer places an instruction book with their product to show how it works. I remember reading a story about someone in the Chicago area who had one of the first Ford motorcars which was produced. Out in the countryside it broke down. He was at a loss to know what to do. Finally another Ford chugged up and a kind and knowledgeable-looking man got out.

"Can I help you, Sir?" he asked with some authority. The owner of the new little Ford was more than happy for any help he could get. The stranger fiddled a few minutes, then turned the crank handle and, lo and behold, the car started!

With great relief the owner of the struggling vehicle, now delighted that it was running, asked the stranger whether he could have his name and address so he could write and thank him and send him a gift. The stranger replied: "I do not wish to give you my address, and there is no need for a letter or a gift. But I am happy to give you my name. My name is Henry Ford."

Henry Ford, who had designed and made the first Ford motorcar knew how it worked and could do the necessary to make it function.

Likewise, God our Heavenly Father in both Old and New Testaments of the Bible has given us guidelines to show how the institution of marriage which He has made central to the well being of humankind can and should work. There are, as I say, a number of steps we need to follow.

Attitude of love
We are to understand that, in terms of biblical norms and standards, there is underway a civil war of values, especially on the family and sexuality levels, and we need to get into it in the right spirit. I believe it is essential as Christians that we do not allow ourselves to be swept away by the prevailing norms of the day. But we must remember, as we resist, to do so with Christian love for those who take a contrary line. Without this love, we lose the battle before it has even begun.

Universal physical and moral laws
We have to grasp by faith and demonstrate in our Christian apologetics that we live in a God-created universe of physical and

moral law. These laws, as noted in the previous chapter, govern everything in our universe. The early scientists grasped this, and sought to uncover the physical laws that God had already put in place. They didn't invent the laws but discovered laws that were already there. Likewise, in the moral arena, laws are also uncovered both in Scripture and through studying what works best in experience. Laws relating to family life, marriage, and sexuality are no exception. If we do not cooperate with these laws, we damage ourselves. In other words, we do not break laws, we just illustrate them as they break us. No one jumping from a tall building breaks the law of gravity; they only illustrate it. Likewise in the moral arena, as we hopefully registered earlier.

The Jesus way in the universe

We need to grasp, as we said in chapter one, that if Jesus is the *Logos* of God who was and is God, and if He is the Creator of the universe (see John 1:3; Colossians 1:17) then the moral fabric of the universe actually stems from Him and is created by Him. This means that there is a Jesus stamp on the universe. It also means that in His teaching on marriage, as on everything else, He did not impose a morality on humans but only exposed more fully and completely an intrinsic morality already in the universe. A good and moral action, therefore, will have not only Jesus and Scripture behind it, but the universe and the cosmos. And a bad or evil action will not only stand under the judgment of God and Scripture, but under the judgement of life and the cosmos. If this is an accurate description of reality, it only remains for us to find out what God's intended way or ways are for sexuality, marriage, and the family.

The Jesus way in marriage

We have to ascertain how the Scriptures generally – and Jesus and the apostles specifically – view the divine way for marriage, family life and sexuality. Not surprisingly, given all we have said above, the divine way is anchored in creation and in a particular and divine intention for the created order. Says Genesis 1:27: "So God created man in his own image, in the image of God he created him; male and female he created them."

As to how this male-female relationship is to work in all its dimensions, including the sexual, is then further elaborated in another creation ordinance found in Genesis 2:24: "Therefore a man leaves his father and his mother and cleaves to his wife, and they become one flesh."

Says Dr Ed Wheat, "These twenty-two words sum up the entire teaching of Scripture on marriage. All else that is said emphasises or amplifies the three fundamental principles originated here (i.e., leave, cleave, become one flesh), *but never* changes them in the slightest."[3] And no other plan or way is given or sanctioned for the expression of intimate inter-personal sexual relationships.

The word of Jesus in Matthew 19:4-6 is also critical as He confirms the Genesis 2:24 principle and sanctions only monogamous heterosexual marriage. Says Jesus, "Have you not read that he who made them *from the beginning* made them *male* and *female*, and said, 'For this reason a man shall leave his father and mother and be joined to his wife, and the two shall become one flesh'? So they are no longer two but one flesh. What therefore God has joined together, let not man put asunder" (italics mine). Here Jesus only affirms the original creation ordinance and design.

The Old and New Testament are in complete harmony on this point. In some cases, as an expression or manifestation of progressive revelation, Jesus says "Moses said to you – a, b, and c. But I say to you x, y, and z." But not on this. He affirms the creation and Mosaic norm for heterosexual marriage and He sanctions no other. His appeal is to the constituted nature of things in the created order, whether physiological, biological, psychological, emotional or social. So is the Apostle Paul's in Romans 1:26-27 where he condemns homosexual practice as "unnatural", i.e., contrary to nature and the natural order (see chapter five).

Non-Jesus options

We have to emphasise to the world around us that non-Jesus options will not work for our fullest happiness. What are these non-Jesus options?

Polygamy

Polygamy was sanctioned in the Old Testament. David and Solomon are two examples of men who basically did what was right in the eyes of the Lord, but who were polygamous. However, Scripture seems to suggest that even Solomon ultimately came to the conclusion that monogamy would be better when in Ecclesiastes 9:9 he instructs the reader to "Enjoy life with the wife [singular, not plural] whom you love."

Certainly via the progressive revelation of the New Testament, we see that monogamy is much more the divine will. In 1 Timothy 3, Paul repeatedly asserts, for example, that Christian leaders should only have one wife, an indication that this is the best and the Jesus way for those God calls to be married.

However, one need not open the Bible to come to this conclusion. I was once speaking in Swaziland to a group of African clergy, and the issue of polygamy arose. Many of these ministers had been brought up in polygamous homes, and I thought many would say, "Polygamy is our way and custom and it is fine." But not one of those ministers was prepared to make a case for polygamy. In fact, many said quite the reverse, that it was an unhappy way which caused nothing but tension, jealousy, heartache and trauma in the household. Their experience said it was not the Jesus way, but rather a way falling far short of God's highest will.

Promiscuity

The Scriptures are very clear that the promiscuity way stands under the judgment of God. Numerous references appear in the Old Testament on this subject, not least of which is the seventh commandment: "You shall not commit adultery" (Exodus 20:14). The Book of Proverbs also forcefully condemns promiscuity, "He who commits adultery has no sense; he who does it destroys himself" (Proverbs 6:32). There are also numerous New Testament references speaking against promiscuity. Hebrews 13:4b is one example: "God will judge the immoral and the adulterous." Promiscuity just does not work as a way of ultimate sexual fulfilment because it does not gladden or satisfy, except briefly. "Stolen waters are sweet", but afterwards they are the way of death. (Proverbs 9:17-18). Having counselled hundreds who have gone this route, I can confirm its futility.

Serial monogamy

Having one marriage partner after another, in the manner of Elizabeth Taylor, who has been married eight times to seven different men, is serial monogamy. But these relationships fail just as miserably as polygamy and promiscuity and usually leave a trail of emotional devastation.

Same-sex civil unions or same-sex marriage

We explore same-sex unions in chapters five and six, where we will see its complete moral eccentricity, novelty and "out-of-line-ness" with any marital norm since humankind began. Nor does any major religion in the world sanction it, other than a minuscule percentage of Christians.

Christian marriage

All of this then leaves us with Christian marriage as the only other option. Daunting perhaps, but less so if we seek to see from Scripture how it is meant to work.

We have to affirm and reaffirm and discover and rediscover, without loss of nerve, the Bible's way for marriage and sexuality. First we have to understand that marriage fulfils God's original creation ordinance and plan and it is the fundamental building block of society. Indeed, the first chapters of Genesis show us that God instituted the home even before the state, school or church. It is a divine creation ordinance, and has nothing to do with humankind's design or plan. And its fourfold purpose is *companionship, mutual help, sexual fulfilment* and *procreation*.

"Therefore a man leaves his father and his mother and cleaves to his wife, and they become one flesh. And the man and his wife were both naked, and were not ashamed" (Genesis 2:24-25). We see here that God's divine pattern for marriage, established as part of creation, produced something extraordinary and, in a way, almost unimaginable. Two people, the man and the woman, become one. This is something more and greater simply than togetherness. It is a mystery indeed which no thinkers, theologians or teachers have ever been able adequately to explain.

Two people become "one flesh". How it takes place we cannot fully fathom or plumb. We just know it happens.

And of course if the two are becoming one in this very deep sense, then it rules out all adultery, unfaithfulness and promiscuity. If the two have become one, that can't then keep happening in half a dozen directions. In fact, the Bible is quite clear on the dreadful consequences of adultery. Thus for example Proverbs 6:32 can say: "He who commits adultery has no sense; he who does it destroys himself."

Having insisted that biblical marriage has to be both monogamous and heterosexual, Ed Wheat writes:

> Although it goes far deeper than the physical, becoming one flesh involves intimate physical union in sexual intercourse. And this without shame between marriage partners. Shame in marital sex was never imparted by God! Instead, the biblical expression for sexual intercourse between husband and wife is *to know*, an expression of profound dignity. "Adam *knew* Eve his wife; and she conceived..." (Genesis 4:1). "Then Joseph ... took unto him his wife: and *knew* her until she had brought forth her firstborn son..." (Matthew 1:24-25).
>
> This word *know* is the same word used of God's loving, personal knowledge of Abraham in Genesis 18:19: "for I *know* him, that he will command his children and his household after him, and they shall keep the way of the Lord, to do justice and judgement..."
>
> Thus, in the divine pattern of marriage, sexual intercourse between husband and wife includes both intimate physical knowledge and a tender, intimate, personal knowledge. So the leaving, cleaving, and knowing each other results in a new identity in which two individuals merge into one – one in mind, heart, body and spirit. This is why divorce has such a devastating effect. Not two people are left, but two fractions of one...
>
> Here then is the marriage design as ordained by God at the very beginning – a love relationship so deep, tender, pure, and intimate that it is patterned after that of Christ for His church. This is the foundation for the love-life you can experience in your own marriage, a foundation on which you can safely build."[4]

So we see God afresh as the author and giver of our sexuality. We did not buy it in a drugstore. It is given to us by God as integral to our humanity and as we receive the Genesis word that Adam "knew" Eve (4:1), so we embrace profoundly the notion that sex, although physical, is primarily a deeply spiritual and emotional communication of one person to another at the deepest possible level.

All this says that marriage and sexuality, inherently good in and of themselves, are given by God to fulfil our various needs as humans. They fulfil our sexual needs, our social needs for companionship, and our character needs whereby we can grow and develop as people. Christian marriage also fulfils the fundamental needs of children. Only a healthy home with a happily married father and mother will provide children with the proper feelings of security to allow for normal psychological and emotional development. Former U.S. President Lyndon Johnson once said wisely in a speech that "the family is the cornerstone of our society. More than any other force it shapes the attitudes, hopes, ambitions and values of the child. When the family collapses it is the children that are usually damaged. When it happens on a massive scale the wider community itself is crippled."

I believe that is so and much modern evidence confirms it. However, the making of a good marriage is a demanding enterprise and will elude us unless we seek earnestly, with the Lord's help, to follow some key guiding biblical principles.

Christ must be at the centre of the marriage

Marriage is basically a spiritual relationship. And while it does address many of our physical, social and emotional needs here on earth, Augustine rightly prays, "Thou hast made us for thyself and our hearts are restless till they find their rest in thee." No spouse can fill that God-shaped vacuum designed only for our Lord himself. If we expect a husband or wife to meet our deepest spiritual needs, he or she will always disappoint us. In fact, such an effort is entirely unfair to our partner and can only lead to disillusionment, frustration and disappointment. Often people will leave a spouse to find someone else whom they think will fill the vacuum. But they can't. Only the Lord can do it. Why? Because the vacuum is God-shaped.

In a sense then, we could say that a successful marriage is really made up of three good marriages, the first to Christ, the second to oneself – for we have to love and value ourselves – and the third to our husband or wife.

Both partners have to seek by the Spirit to act in love to each other

Love is not just a feeling, but an action, a way of behaving, in fact a commitment. In other words, love *does* certain things and makes us become certain kinds of people. The problem of marriage is not just finding the right partner, but being the right partner by both words and deeds. Demanding, yes, but highly rewarding when we succeed and certainly painful when we fail.

The four loves

Now we must note something very key. The "marriage carriage" is drawn not by one horse but by four, as captured by four Greek words:

- *Eros,* which speaks of romantic and sexual love;
- *Philea,* which is love as friendship, having fun and sharing common interests;
- *Storge,* which is affection, warmth and tender familiarity; and
- *Agape,* which is God's "in-spite-of" love, i.e., love as action, behaviour and commitment.

It is especially important to distinguish between *eros* and *agape*. *Eros* is full of great feelings, as opposed to *agape* which is full of great demands. *Eros* can scale great heights, while *agape* can carry us through great depths. *Eros* gets things started but cannot cope with the long haul all by itself. *Eros* makes promises of "undying love forever", but it cannot keep them without the help of *agape*. Then while *eros* has its centre of gravity in the human couple together, *agape* includes both mutual responsibility to one another but also a further responsibility to God as the indispensable third party from whom the grace and capacity for *agape* really comes. In fact, C.S. Lewis notes that sustained *agape* love can keep *eros* love alive and flourishing.[5]

So, too, while *eros* speaks of being in love, *agape* speaks of loving. It includes the will, and the determination and resolution to loyalty as the Lord helps us. *Agape* knows that even in the best relationships and marriages there are times when romantic love ebbs, and loyalty and commitment must fill the gap. These two are not opposites, but complementary "twins" in every good marriage.

Writes C.S. Lewis: "The loves prove that they are unworthy to take the place of God by the fact that they cannot even remain themselves and do what they promise to do without God's help."[6]

The great Swiss marriage counsellor, Theodor Bovet, while speaking of God's *agape*, in-spite -of love, puts it this way:

> Sex has its centre of gravity in the ego; Eros has its centre of gravity in "us two" – the human couple; Agape's centre of gravity lies beyond the human couple. Agape includes mutual responsibility, but also a further responsibility to a third party. It maintains loyalty between couples even when one party no longer desires to be loyal. "Fall but in love with me, loyal thou needst not be", sings Eros. But Agape knows that even in the best marriages there can be times when love ebbs and loyalty has to fill the gap.

> Agape, as Brunner says, loves the other because he exists, not because of certain characteristics. A man loves his wife, not just her beautiful face; a woman loves her husband, not just his intellect. Thus Agape is not tied to sexual differentiation like sex and Eros. "There is no more male nor female, but all are one in Christ Jesus." So, too, Agape is the basis of friendship.[7]

Bovet then adds:

> But it would be a gross mistake to set up Agape and Eros against each other as two mutually exclusive opposites, or as though Agape was nobler and more 'Christian' than Eros. Both are necessary elements in any good marriage. Every good marriage must be a friendship as well as a marriage. Husband and wife must think as much of each other, love each other, interest each other, just as much as two really good friends. But woe to the marriage that is only a friendship, only Agape! In every good marriage, too, husband and wife must love each other as passionately, go on making each other as happy, go on being as new a surprise to each other, as any pair of lovers who are 'mad about each other'. But woe to the marriage that is only passion, only Eros![8]

A further and useful point in this regard is made by Ed Wheat:

By the way, there can be no such thing as window shopping here. You cannot pick and choose the kind of love you prefer and discard the others. Each builds on the other. Each has its own special, significant place, as you will find when you begin putting all these loves into practice in your marriage. But if they are quite distinctive, they are also interrelated so that the physical, emotional, and spiritual processes overlap and reinforce each other in the act of loving.[9]

That said, there are a couple of other points to make.

Prayer must be integral to our marriage relationships

Prayer is a mighty marital bonding force as we together bring our problems, sorrows, joys and tensions to the Lord. Also as we bring to him the spiritual and other needs of our children, loved ones and friends. In prayer we also confess our hurts or offences to one another and seek forgiveness.

In fact, mutual forgiveness has to become a way of life and we should seek to heed the injunction, "...do not let the sun go down on your anger" (Ephesians 4:26). Two of the toughest but sweetest words in any good marriage are "I'm sorry" and we can even say them while praying together!

Mutual submission

Although Scripture assigns a servant, sacrificial and deeply loving and caring headship in marriage to the husband (Colossians 3:18; Ephesians 5:23-24), whereby the husband has an ultimate accountability to God for his family, and especially its spiritual life, this does not mean that in all details and aspects the husband leads and decides. Indeed, in the day-to-day affairs and processes of the marriage, who decides and leads in this or that will depend both on the persons and situations involved in the life of the couple. The key thing here is that the husband's leadership is clearly set in the context firstly of the husband sacrificially loving his wife with the depth and sacrificial care that "Christ loved the Church and gave himself up for her" (Ephesians 5:25) and, secondly, both of them living in mutual submission "to one another" (Ephesians 5:21). There is to be a caring and mutually submissive give-and-take in the godly interplay of husband and wife in Christian marriage.

An obvious corollary of the above therefore is that it is a travesty and abuse of the "headship" principle when ungodly men use this sensitively tuned principle to abuse their wives, dominate or lord it over them, or inflict damage on them. This is a million light-years from what the scriptures are on about when they say "the husband is the head of the wife" (Ephesians 5:23). For husbands to grasp the true meaning of this requires revisiting Calvary, sitting at the foot of the Cross and drinking in the spirit of sacrifice.

We have to be the right kind of parents and the right kind of example

Agreement on how to raise our children (e.g., Ephesians 6:4) and also on how to be good parents (1 Timothy 3:12) is also crucial, not to mention the example we set them. Individual time is also a must for our kids. Delinquent and over-busy fathers need especially to register this. The emotional and sexual development of a daughter is generally greatly influenced by how well her father's love and tenderness are expressed to her. And dads taking quality time with their sons is a source of immense blessing to both. Indeed, children growing up in a healthy and happy home where there is love and mutual care all round can count themselves blessed indeed.

Conclusion

Marriage is a precious gift of God and therefore to be cherished, guarded and societally protected. Sadly, as marriage comes increasingly under attack and as more and more marriages fail, the Jesus way seems to stand a smaller and smaller chance of becoming the prevailing way of life in the world today. But I believe we can say that, if marriage and the home are allowed to collapse, then the moral fabric of society will be irreparably damaged and sadness on an epic scale will engulf us. Also, the ethics and morals of all other areas of life are likely to spiral downward perilously at an ever-increasing speed.

So let us all try, with the Lord's help, to preach, propagate and work out the Judaeo-Christian and Jesus way for marriage and family life. The alternatives are certainly not working or bringing wholeness and happiness. Maybe it is time once again to let Jesus have his way with us in this most blessed and precious of human relationships.

Writing in *Christian Living Today*, a South African Christian magazine, my daughter Deborah Kirsten writes about her marriage to Gary and says:

> Until our hearts are touched and we experience intimacy, we are but shadows of our real selves. We were born and created for intimacy, firstly with our Creator, then with ourselves and then with others. …What has made an astounding difference to our lives and our capacity to connect to one another is our ability and desire to connect first and foremost with our Creator.
>
> As you pursue intimacy, don't try and attempt to find in another human being the intimacy you were meant to find in a relationship with Jesus Christ. Ultimately, our full craving for intimacy will only be realised when our hearts touch God Himself. "Indeed we are but shadows … *till the heart be touched*", and we were but shadows until God breathed life into us. Then He engineered the great human connection: "Two shall become one."
>
> And humankind discovered the great possibility: Two hearts can touch. That's intimacy.[10]

Yes! And that's marriage.

End Notes

1. James Davison Hunter, *Culture Wars – The Struggle to Define America: Making sense of the battles over the family, art, education, law and politics* (San Francisco: Basic Books, 1991), 176.

2. David P. Gushee, "A Crumbling Institution – How Social Resolutions Cracked the Pillars of Marriage", *Christianity Today* (September 2004): 42-45.

3. Ed Wheat, *Love Life for Every Married Couple* (Vereeniging, South Africa: Christian Art Publishers, 1980), 27.

4. Wheat, 32-33, italics his.

5. C.S. Lewis, *The Four Loves* (London & Glasgow: Fontana Books, 1960); see chapter 6.

6. Lewis, 109.

7. Theodor Bovet, *A Handbook to Marriage* (Garden City, New York: Dolphin Books, 1958), 27.

8. Bovet, 27-28.

9. Wheat, 58.

10. Deborah Kirsten, "Till the Heart Be Touched", *Christian Living Today* (December 2004/January 2005): 11.

Chapter Three

Divorce – The Great Tragedy

Having opened these reflections with a broad discussion on how the Christian should approach ethics generally, we began moving into more specific areas, beginning with some thoughts on what constitutes a healthy Christian marriage. I want now to tackle the delicate, sensitive and vexed issue of divorce. I do so with some trepidation and with an open confession that I will no doubt leave numerous loose ends. Even so, I want to try and proceed with a continued emphasis on the Jesus way as one built by Him as the agent in creation into the moral fabric of the created order. We also approach the issue with Jesus and the Scriptures as our supreme authority and guide. That is always my basic presupposition. I feel that if we depart from that we are completely at sea. Look at much of the contemporary church and you'll know what I mean.

The Christian concept of marriage

I once wrote to John Stott, the great evangelical leader in England, to get his thoughts on the subject of divorce. In his response to me he wrote as follows:

> The first thing I try to say to people who approach me on this issue is that I never talk about divorce without having previously talked about two other subjects. The first is marriage. Every Christian must assert that God's purpose in marriage was that it should be a permanent and exclusive union, and that this was confirmed by Jesus in his well-known phrase, "What God has joined together, let no man put asunder" (Matthew 19:6). Even if divorce under certain circumstances is permissible, as I believe it is, it is nevertheless always second best and the result of human sin. It is not commanded in Scripture, only permitted as a concession. The second prior subject on which I would want to speak is reconciliation. The Christian religion is in its very essence a religion of peace and reconciliation. Even if divorce is permitted, no Christian would consider it unless his or her conscience is clear that he or she has done everything possible to seek a reconciliation.[1]

This seems to me fundamental. Divorce is not some legal or religious luxury which opens the gate to green pastures of romantic bliss and emotional freedom, but rather a tragedy of major proportions which should be utterly avoided unless the situation is completely and irrevocably irretrievable and beyond redemption.

Having said that, we must also immediately add that, because God is alive, and because "all authority in heaven and on earth" (Matthew 28:18) is vested in Jesus and the Holy Spirit, no situation in itself need be irreparably lost. The age of miracles is not over. And there are many Christian couples who can testify to God having wrought the most miraculous healings in the most hopeless of marital situations. In our African Enterprise work we have seen this any number of times.

God's original intention and biblical grounds for divorce

As I said, I touch this subject with some trembling because it is so fraught with complication and pain for so many. But we must try to grapple with the biblical data in sincerity and humility. First of all we must understand that the whole weight of both Old and New Testament teaching is that God intended marriage to be permanent and indissoluble. Said Jesus, "What therefore God has joined together, let not man put asunder" (Matthew 19:4-6; Mark 10:6-9). That original divine intent remains the perfect, unchanging model. God's original intention of marriage permanence continues as the present ideal.

Secondly, both in the Old and New Testaments, provisions for divorce are made. These are not to be viewed as easy loopholes for lightly terminating a marriage alliance. Rather they are taking into account the exceptional dilemmas in which sinful humans sometimes find themselves. Divorce is thus a concession to that human "hardness of heart", as Jesus put it (Matthew 19:7-8), which frustrates God's highest and best will. For this reason, it incurs God's grave disapproval, and in Malachi 2:16 we have the Lord's verdict, "I hate divorce". But, that said, divorce can also be a rare provision under certain circumstances to dissolve a bond which, within the tragedy of human existence, has become a travesty of the divine intention in marriage.

God therefore grants the divorce concession, his original intent having now become subject to His permissive and conditional will for a sinful and failing humankind. In other words, God is recognising that sin creates certain necessities and some dreadful situations which must be dealt with, but they must be dealt with very much against the backdrop of what He originally intended and planned – namely the indissolubility of marriage.

It is this original intention which has properly led the Church down through history to take a strong line against divorce. On the other hand, in the chaos, confusion and neo-paganism of a secularist post-Christian era, the Church has recognised the right of the state to frame its own divorce laws, and many Christians have recognised that the "irretrievable breakdown" concept may be the best and fairest basis for legislation in a secular, post-Christian society, especially where the people concerned do not have a Christian commitment or a concern for biblical faithfulness.

The Church, however, has to try midst all the ambiguities and complexities of marital and sexual chaos in the twenty-first century to maintain its own witness and encourage its own members to apply the biblical bases of divorce at least in their own ranks as best they can, thereby seeking to influence society at large.

Needless to say, there is no reference in the Bible to any divorce provisions for same-sex marriages, as the whole notion of such a union is biblically unthinkable in the first place. (This subject will be examined in chapter six).

The New Testament recognises two grounds for divorce, adultery and desertion.

Adultery

The Greek word for adultery, *porneia* (Matthew 5:31 and 19:9) basically refers to sexual infidelity and "every kind of unlawful sexual intercourse" (Arndt and Gingrich Greek Lexicon). This would certainly include adultery, even though the exact Greek word for adultery (*moicheia*) is not used here.

This one sin, above all others, violates the "one-flesh" principle which is fundamental to marriage and thereby disrupts the marital bond. This is not to say that sexual unfaithfulness automatically dissolves a marriage, but it creates a biblically legitimate basis to do so. In other words, divorce for adultery is permissible, though not mandatory. The preferred course following unfaithfulness obviously is repentance and reconciliation towards both God and one's partner and the receiving of forgiveness from both. There is, of course, also pastoral ministry required for the third party.

In his comprehensive and strong book, *Divorce and Remarriage*, Andrew Cornes writes: "God originally made humans male and female with a view to marriage; at the beginning of creation he instituted marriage: an event (it *is* also a process but Christ is speaking here about what happens at the moment a man marries a woman) when each partner leaves his/her original family, forms a new family with the partner to whom he/she cleaves, and – most importantly – is made 'one' with his/her partner. It is God who joins the couple together as one. The implication is obvious: no one is to sunder this God-given oneness (Mark 10:6-9; Matthew 19:4-6)."[2]

The clear corollary of this is that divorce can never be part of God's primary will, because it is God's will that the one-flesh oneness should not only exist but be lived out in marital fidelity. Jesus does, however, permit – not command – divorce in the case of adultery, and seemingly in that one case only.

Cornes then goes on to make the point, which would probably be very difficult for many today, that legal divorce does in one sense not destroy the one-flesh oneness of the first marriage. Couples "can undo their own work (of getting legally married); they cannot undo the work of God" in giving them that original oneness through the physical and sexual union of marriage.[3]

The reason for this is that, in the divine structure and scheme of things, when a man and a woman come together in sexual intercourse, the union is not just physical, but profoundly spiritually uniting and divinely bonding. The marriage bond is not just a human contract but involves a divine "joining together" because God has glued them, cemented them and "yoked them together" (the literal meaning in Matthew 19:5-6). We should note that, in verse 5, Jesus speaks of the man and the woman being joined together, but in verse 6 He says "*what* (not those) therefore God has joined together let not man put asunder." The *what* He is speaking of is the divinely created yoke – namely the marriage relationship itself – whereby, like two yoked animals pulling a load together, the man and the woman take upon themselves this yoke so that together they can share the loads of life and achieve what neither of them could achieve alone. This yoke, this marriage relationship, no one should damage, smash or "put asunder". (The Greek word used here – *chorizo* – means divide, separate, sever, sunder, split apart.) Why? Because it is God's intention that the marriage relationship be permanent and continue as long as both parties are alive.

Says William Barclay: "The ideal is that in the marriage state two people find the completing of their personalities."[4]

So now, what about divorce? When asked by the Pharisees about Moses "commanding" divorce (Matthew 19:7) though they conveniently ignore Moses' giving a *basis* for divorce (Hebrew: *erwat dabar* – some indecency), Jesus replied that it was not a "command", but a "permission" (Matthew 19:8). And He gave human stubbornness or "hardness of heart" (v. 8) as the reason for the Mosaic permission, even though this violated the divine intention, because "from the beginning it was not so" (v. 8). There was here no divine approval of divorce, but only a divine concession, seeing that, for Jesus, what Moses said was what God said. In other words, the divine concession for divorce was nevertheless contrary to the divinely intended plan for marriage. So there is a call, in effect, to go back to the beginning and follow God's original intention.

At which point Jesus stated to them His ruling on this matter: "And I say to you, whoever divorces his wife, except for unchastity, and marries another, commits adultery" (Matthew 19:9; cf. Matthew 5:31-32). This is the famous so-called "exceptive clause" whose validity stands in spite of Mark and Luke omitting it in their Gospel accounts. On this John Stott comments: "Nor is its omission in Mark and Luke a sufficient reason for rejecting it as a Matthean interpretation, representing (perhaps) the view of the Palestinian Church within which the first gospel came to be written. The silence of Mark and Luke need not be explained as due to their ignorance of the exceptive clause; it may equally well have been due to their taking it for granted. For everybody (including both schools of Hillel and Shammai) was agreed that adultery was a legitimate ground for divorce. This was not in dispute."[5]

So Jesus permitted divorce for adultery because it violates the "one-flesh" principle that is intrinsic, fundamental and at the heart of marriage as divinely ordained and biblically defined. But it was the only ground He gave for terminating the marriage.

This was tough for His disciples to hear amidst the divorce laxity prevalent at the time. Some of the leading Jewish scholars and rabbis (e.g., Akiba and Hillel) were diluting even the Mosaic teaching on this and permitting divorce on the most trifling grounds, thereby incurring His castigating comment that they were "making void the word of God through your tradition which you hand on. And many such things you do" (Mark 7:13).

Not surprisingly, the startled and daunted disciples, on hearing Jesus' standard and ideal, respond: "'If such is the case of a man with his wife, it is not expedient to marry.' But he said to them, 'Not all men can receive this saying, but only those to whom it is given. For there are eunuchs who have been so from birth, and there are eunuchs who have been made eunuchs by men, and there are eunuchs who have made themselves eunuchs for the sake of the kingdom of heaven. He who is able to receive this, let him receive it.'" (Matthew 19:10-12). Says William Barclay: "Jesus says quite clearly that not everyone can in fact accept this situation, that only those to whom it has been granted to do so can accept this saying. What Jesus is really saying is this – *only the Christian can accept the Christian ethic*. Only the man who has the continual help of Jesus Christ and the continual guidance of the Holy Spirit can build up the personal relationship which the ideal of marriage demands. Only by the help of Jesus Christ can a man develop the sympathy, the understanding, the forgiving spirit, the considerate love, which true marriage requires. Without the help of Jesus Christ these things are plainly impossible. The Christian ideal of marriage involves the prerequisite that the partners to marriage are Christian. No one can live out Jesus Christ's teaching without Jesus Christ… The teaching of Christ demands the presence of Christ."[6]

Let me comment on the mysterious reference here to eunuchs. A eunuch is a man who is unsexed, in one of three ways: (1) either by some deformity, or inherited sterility or physical imperfection; or (2) by castration, as happened in the ancient world frequently to palace servants, for example, those looking after a royal harem; or (3) by a voluntary surrendering of love, sex and marriage for a spiritual reason (i.e., the Kingdom of God). There are people who have chosen this way in order to be obedient to a call of God, or to fulfil a ministry in a place too dangerous or insecure for marriage to be manageable. Others, like some I know, out of theological conviction, have declined to remarry after divorce feeling that to do so would compromise their convictions regarding remarriage following divorce. The Lord seems aware that some will be able "to accept this", others not.

But yes, if there has been adultery, divorce is permissible. It is the only ground Jesus allows. And He knew many would struggle to accept it. But those who could accept it should.

Desertion

When we step into the world of Paul, we find, however, a second basis of divorce in the New Testament, namely desertion. But we should note that for him, as for Jesus, the first word on the subject is that there should for Christians be no divorce. Says Paul: "the wife should not separate from her husband" (1 Corinthians 7:10) and "the husband should not divorce his wife" (1 Corinthians 7:11). But Paul introduces one exception, and that is if there is desertion. This relates to the context where two non-Christians marry, one of whom is subsequently converted, and then, for whatever reason the Christian finds himself or herself in a "mixed marriage" and married to an unbeliever who then deserts the marriage.

In 1 Corinthians 7, Paul addresses three categories of people: First "the unmarried and widows" (vv. 8,9), then "the married" (vv. 10,11), then "the rest" (vv. 12-16), the context showing he has in mind a particular kind of "mixed marriage" (i.e., believer to unbeliever).

Presumably the Corinthians had asked Paul about such problems which had arisen in Corinth. His reply was that if the unbelieving partner "consents to live" with the believer, the believer should on no account divorce the unbeliever (1 Corinthians 7:12-13). This means that Christian conversion, as some Corinthians thought, does not affect the basic marriage bond which should not be broken. They should not divorce (1 Corinthians 7:12,13). Only death dissolves the marriage bond (1 Corinthians 7:39). "But if the unbelieving partner desires to separate, let it be so; in such a case the brother or sister is not bound. For God has called us to peace" (1 Corinthians 7:15).

We need to register here that the believer's freedom to disengage from the marriage is not due to the believer's conversion (as noted above) but to the unbelieving partner's resistance to the Gospel and unwillingness to remain in the marriage. The believer will resist divorce proceedings, but if this fails, they may acquiesce in the unbeliever's determination to terminate the marriage.

In other words, if a Christian believer is deserted by his or her unbelieving partner, then reluctantly and sadly, having failed to win that partner to Christ, the believer is permitted to acquiesce in the desertion, secure a divorce and presumably, according to the judgement of most scholars, remarry "only in the Lord" (1 Corinthians 7:39), i.e., to a fellow believer.

Any other grounds for the 21st century?

This is tricky. And I tremble to touch it. But let's at least note that the grounds God allowed through Moses (*erwat dabar* – "some indecency") and the grounds Jesus mentioned explaining the Mosaic grounds (*porneia* – "sexual immorality"), relate to *different kinds of sexual sin or perversion* and not adultery alone. This being so, maybe, as some would argue, this could include some grounds beyond adultery.[7]

I am not personally sure, but might this cover a man seeking bizarre types of sex from his wife, or getting into perversion, or incest, or having pornographic "affairs" via the internet, or physically and sexually abusing his children, sometimes violently? This latter is very common now in South Africa. And it's an acute pastoral problem. How should pastors out there in the real world, not of theory but grim reality, advise people?

Bishop Frank Retief of Cape Town, while stressing the contractual and covenantal nature of marriage in biblical times, asks: "If marriage is a legal contract between two people to love, comfort, honour and keep each other, in sickness and in health, forsaking all others, as long as they both live, when is it broken? Loving companionship is broken when abuse, adultery or abandonment enter the marriage in any of their many forms."[8]

He adds: "The sixth commandment says: 'You shall not murder'. The word 'murder' is used as a figure of speech to cover all forms of violence. Physical violence breaks the sixth commandment. Sin is committed and the covenant of companionship dishonoured. It is absolutely unbiblical for any marriage to be violent or for you to stay in a home where violence is present. As a Christian, you have an obligation to seek protection for yourself and your children if your husband is violent. It is your responsibility to retreat from such a situation."[9]

Retief, a bishop with strong evangelical and biblical commitments, goes on to note that "God places a high value on womanhood and on peace and harmony in the home. Abuse, slander and insults break the marriage contract, as does the unpredictable, uncaring behaviour of a spouse. We saw in Deuteronomy 24:4 that if a wife was accused of indecency, the law provided for a legal divorce and remarriage. She was entitled to retreat and not to take up the option of a reconciliation because of the unpredictability of her husband. God hates divorce (Malachi 2:16), but that is not all he hates. God hates a man who treats his wife cruelly and then, when his rage subsides and he feels remorse, wants to have sex with her. This is unacceptable. A situation of ongoing violence and strife breaks the marriage contract and the woman should retreat. God has called us to live in peace (1 Corinthians 7:15). If this condition does not prevail in your home, you should retreat."[10]

The notion here is that if a marital situation becomes so bad, evil, demeaning and destructive, even dangerous, that it is more sinful to stay in it than to get out of it, even for one's children's sake, then it becomes advisable if not imperative to move out of it. We need to be honest and acknowledge that some biblically committed pastors would only sanction moving out and relocating away from the abusive spouse, as it were – i.e., a "separation" – but not formal divorce.

Others, on the other hand, would say the covenantal and contractual nature of the marriage has already been shattered by such behaviour and the marriage ought therefore to be dissolved by divorce with the right of the innocent party to remarry. The issue is vexed and I suspect we do not do one another a service if we pretend otherwise. Nor is the best pastoral approach in handling the issue always clear (more on this in the next chapter).

Summary

To sum up, the basic biblical view is that, while marriage is intended by God to be permanent, it may be dissolved either on the grounds of sexual unfaithfulness or desertion of a Christian believer by a non-Christian partner, leaving innocent parties free to remarry. But only if all efforts at reconciliation (1 Corinthians 7:11) and peace (1 Corinthians 7:15) have been exhausted. Inevitably, different denominations and pastors apply both the letter and the spirit of Scripture differently within the wide range of human complexities and pastoral needs concerning this subject. But I believe we will serve both people and the Church best by seeking to apply the biblical principles as faithfully as we are able. How we do this we'll turn to in our next chapter, as well as the complex question of remarriage.

End Notes

1. Personal letter from John Stott to the author.
2. Andrew Cornes, *Divorce and Remarriage*
   (London: Hodder & Stoughton, 1993), 234, italics his.
3. Cornes, 235.
4. William Barclay, *The Gospel of Matthew – Vol. 2*
   (Edinburgh: The Saint Andrew Press, 1967), 224.
5. John Stott, *Divorce* (London: Falcon Books, 1972), 9.
6. Barclay, 227-228.
7. For a more extensive discussion of this, see *True Sexual Morality
   – Recovering Biblical Standards for a Culture in Crisis*
   by Daniel R. Heimbach (Wheaton, Illinois: Crossway Books, 2004),
   204-207.
8. Frank J. Retief, *Divorce – Hope for the Hurting* (Cape Town:
   Struik Christian Books, 1990), 78-79.
9. Retief, 79.
10. Retief, 79.

Chapter Four

DIVORCE – APPLYING THEOLOGY AND PRINCIPLES

As we proceed further into this difficult issue, we continue to keep in mind the two clear biblical grounds for divorce – namely sexual infidelity and the desertion of a Christian partner by a non-Christian partner – remembering again that this is to be considered against the backdrop of God's basic and original intention for marriage, namely its indissolubility. Let's hold on to that.

Views on divorce

However, the application of this within the general and now-chaotic laxity of twenty-first century marital and sexual patterns, is fraught with problems. Perhaps there are three views to consider.

No compromise

The first stance might be described as "no compromise". When queried as to whether the New Testament standard is enforceable in the late twentieth century, those holding this view would plead that there should be no relaxation at all of the New Testament standards to accommodate the times, because this is Jesus' clear teaching and will, and disobedience to it will land the marriage estate in an even worse place. Holders of this view would insist that the church is not to be remoulded or refashioned into the ways and patterns of the world. Says Paul: "Do not be conformed to this world" (Romans 12:2).

Thus can Andrew Cornes write:

> Yet sadly the church has in fact "conformed" to the world in this century, in the sexual and marital sphere; or more precisely, limped along behind the world. If liberal secular thought has accepted pre-marital sex and even advocated it, many in the church – both among its leaders and among its ordinary members – have at least become resigned to it, and perhaps been prepared to argue for it, a decade or so later.

But instead, the church's calling is to mould and remake the world, to help the world listen to the teaching of Christ, to encourage the world to obey Christ. The striking fact is that the church has achieved this before now, precisely in the area of sexual and marital morals. The church of the first centuries brought about a sexual and marital revolution within the society of its day. To admire that courage, to marvel at that achievement, to aspire to emulate that influence is not to justify everything that was taught in the early church – of course it had its extremes, both in teaching and in practice – but it is to point out the extraordinary power of Christian ideas and moral standards, and the transformation of society they can bring about. If it can be argued that these were new ideas bursting on the Graeco-Roman world and that Christian teaching could not have the same effect on societies that have been exposed to the New Testament already, we must answer that our own society is almost entirely ignorant of Christian teaching about marriage and singleness, and that if it were forcefully and persuasively presented, it would explode like a bombshell on Western society today and could have the same transforming effect.[1]

This may not be easy. But what if we were to try?

Let me tell you of an interesting and instructive situation. It relates to Christians in Egypt. In our African Enterprise ministry we have had numerous and major opportunities for ministry in Egypt. Whenever there, I have been intrigued by the fact that the Egyptian churches, certainly the evangelical ones, simply do not sanction divorce. Instead of making it easy for believers who have marital difficulties to divorce, they in point of fact make it incredibly difficult. Their line is to preach the indissolubility of marriage and to instruct couples to work out their problems. Church leaders there feel that, with the marital and domestic situation being very chaotic in the Muslim world, they need to have a very clear, contrary, positive and contrasting Christian testimony. So, unless in the most dire circumstances, they basically do not allow divorce.

Now the interesting thing is this. Faced with this kind of posture and decree, Egyptian Christian couples whose marriages are in trouble hang in there and work it all out. And homes stay together. One pastor of a big church said to us during our mission to Alexandria: "We have only had three divorces in this congregation in the last forty years." The lesson here is that if the biblical teaching about divorce is really taken seriously, and people know there are no ways out, then they do in fact settle down and make a go of it and resolve their difficulties and by and large come out with happy, satisfactory and lasting marriages. I wouldn't be so bold as to say that there were no unhappy marriages amongst Christians in Egypt, but those in that category put the Lord's rulings on this matter ahead of their personal happiness and they tough it out. And a real measure of contentment arrives. However, the majority who are in marital tension do come through at the end of all their labours and determination to happy and satisfactory marriages for which their children bless them.

Maggie Gallagher, president of the Institute for Marriage and Public Policy in the U.S., says that research indicates that the majority of "unhappily married couples who stick it out" do not "stay miserable". She writes: "The latest data show that within five years, just 12 percent of very unhappily married couples who stick it out are still unhappy; 70 percent of the unhappiest couples now describe their marriage as 'very' or 'quite' happy. Just as good marriages go bad, bad marriages go good. And they have a better chance of doing so in a society that recognizes the value of marriage than one that sings the statistically dubious joys of divorce."[2]

Having said all this, those who take this strong and uncompromising line on marriage with the posture of basically ruling out divorce, except for adultery, would also indeed plead for compassionate understanding and pastoral care for all ensnared by marital disruption.

However, we need to note that people holding this view pose three very important questions. First, what right have we in any way to adapt God's laws to shifting human opinions and sinful practices? Surely in the midst of human relativity, God's laws must nevertheless stand as the permanent standard.

Secondly, did not Christ, the apostles and the early Christian Church face a world with a moral and marital laxity equal to, or even worse than, that of our times? Yet they proceeded on the strict basis established in the New Testament, thereby rescuing the family principle for subsequent centuries. It is also worth noting that despite the fact that classical and pagan Corinth, for example, had no tradition of "covenant" (e.g., God and his people, man and wife, etc.) as existed in the Israelite tradition, nevertheless Paul preached clearly and unashamedly the covenant principle in Christian marriage. So too in Ephesians and Colossians, etc.

Thirdly, who knows better what is good for human beings than God who created us "male and female" and established marriage in the first place as an indissoluble union? It is also true that plain covenantal commitment, when divorce is not seen as an option, as with the Christians in Egypt to whom we have referred, will generally see a couple through enormous difficulties which would have sunk any one else without that commitment.

Beyond that, we have to ask couples about their vows. Did they not, after all, take profoundly solemn vows before God and society to love and cherish one another "for better, for worse, for richer, for poorer, in sickness and in health till death do us part"? Such vows are deeply serious and binding. And the couple taking them should have registered that the wisdom of the ages acknowledges that every marriage has the "for worse" times along with the "for better". Should they now not weather this "for worse" season and somehow negotiate together this season of stormy waters and pain, knowing that the "for better" will return?

Moreover, if they are Christians, are they not one "one in Christ" and bonded in Holy Spirit union with Him? Can this not help them come through this crisis, sharing as they do the mind of Christ (Philippians 2:1-6) and the indwelling Holy Spirit (Romans 8:2-11)?

Moderate accommodation

A second stance might be described as moderate accommodation. Those holding this view would see an impossibility in the present, totally chaotic situation for Christians to enforce a view of no compromise. Yet they would still strongly encourage the marital bond to be maintained even in severe adversity or difficulty. Those taking this line would note that, although Jesus virtually forbade divorce and presented indissolubility as God's absolute, nevertheless because of the sinfulness of human nature He was forced to fix a divorce law at a lower level than the absolute. The question would be: "Why?"

Answer: "To come to terms with the actual and real situation around Him at the time." Thus today, when our actual situation is so totally snarled up, chaotic and ruptured, we must legislate, say those holding this view, the best combination of Christian discipline and mercy, lest worse evils enter the situation. Protagonists of this view would note that countries which have exceptionally strict divorce laws do not necessarily escape the great social problems of adultery, bigamy, illegitimacy, promiscuity and marital breakdown.

William Barclay takes this kind of line, commenting on the Matthew 19 passage:

> We may at the beginning note one thing. *What Jesus laid down was a principle and not a law.* To fail to remember that, and to turn this saying of Jesus into a law, is gravely to misunderstand it. The Bible does not give us *laws*; it gives us *principles* which we must prayerfully and intelligently apply to any given situation. Of the Sabbath the Bible says, 'In it thou shalt not do any work' (Exodus 20:10). In point of fact we know that a complete cessation of work was never possible in any civilization. In an agricultural civilization cattle had still to be tended, and cows had to be milked no matter what the day was. In a developed civilization certain public services must go on, or transport will stand still, water, and light, and heat will not be available. In any home, especially where there are children, there has to be a certain amount of work. A principle can never be quoted as a final law; a principle must always be applied to the individual situation, as God Himself would have it to be applied ... we must take the words of Jesus as a principle which we will apply to the individual cases as they meet us.[3]

Barclay then goes on to urge us, while holding on to the ideal of marriage as an indissoluble union, to register that

> life is not, and never can be, a completely tidy and orderly business. Into life there is bound to come sometimes the element of the unpredictable and the unforcastable. Suppose, then, that two people

enter into the marriage relationship; suppose they do so with the highest hopes and the highest ideals; and then suppose that something unaccountable goes wrong, and that that relationship which should be life's greatest joy becomes hell upon earth ... are then these two people to be told that they are for ever fettered together in a situation which cannot do other than bring a lifetime of misery to both. It is extremely difficult to see how such reasoning can be called Christian; it is extremely hard to see Jesus legalistically condemning two people to any such situation. This is not to say that divorce should be made easy, but it is to say that when all the physical and mental and spiritual resources have been brought to bear on such a situation, and the situation remains incurable and even dangerous, then the situation should be ended, and the Church, so far from regarding people who have been involved in such a situation as being beyond the pale, should do everything it can in strength and tenderness to help them. There does not seem to be any other way than that in which to bring the real Spirit of Christ to bear on the situation.[4]

The compassionate yet scholarly heart of Barclay is speaking. Is he compromising? Is he simply realistic? Is he interpreting the letter of Jesus' words against the backdrop of Jesus' spirit? These are matters with which all concerned Christians have to wrestle.

In any event, four criteria are advanced for the "moderate accommodation" posture:

- The necessity of fixing the law as near the absolute as possible without provoking worse evils.
- The protection of innocent people who might be involved, especially children.
- The need for divorce laws to be reasonably enforceable.
- The advisability at times of separation, even if the course of divorce is not pursued.

Pastoral discretion

A third stance involves what one might call pastoral discretion. The argument goes like this: When Paul allowed a Christian partner to acquiesce in his or her desertion or divorce by an unbelieving partner, he went beyond anything Jesus had said or intimated. In other words, he did not argue for formal retention of the marriage at any cost. Instead he said: "let it be so; in such a case the brother or sister is not bound. For God has called us to peace" (1 Corinthians 7:15).

Proponents of this view see Paul exercising pastoral discretion on a pastoral question and introducing a scale of relative values. While indissoluble marriage alone conforms to God's original intent, personal peace under God featured more highly than retention of a dead or farcical relationship. Better such a marriage be dissolved than that people should be sacrificed on the altar of a totally destructive relationship.

In other words, in some instances, recognised by mature pastoral discretion, divorce and remarriage, even if not for adulterers, may serve the higher good. In this case, what the philosophers call "the tragic moral choice" may be made in the direction of the lesser of two evils, while trusting in God's divine compassion for His blundering creation.

Thus the pastor, following the example of Paul's handling of the Corinthian problems related to believing or unbelieving partners, will counsel extreme situations in the context of what seems spiritually best or the lesser of evils for the individuals concerned. With the transcendent grace and mercy of God placed above absolute and inflexible law, the pastor, exercising pastoral discretion, will face each case on an individual basis.

In this view, the breakdown for which divorce seems the solution speaks of failure to meet God's standards and is therefore a manifestation of human sin. Consequently, all parties need God's grace. But to all divorced persons – guilty as well as innocent – renewing and restoring grace is available on the condition of true penitence, confession and the sincere desire to obey God and fulfil his purpose in the future.

The problem with this view, attractive as it is, is that it can open the floodgates not only to easy or casual marriage and ill-considered divorce, but to over-hasty remarriage, which in turn will often also end in divorce, with the problems which wrecked the first marriage in all likelihood reappearing to wreck the second. Research confirms this.

Guidance

So what are we to say? Of these three options – no compromise, moderate accommodation, and pastoral discretion – my own heart embraces much in two and three, while my head and my Scriptural commitments tend to option one as truest to the Word of God. May the Lord give you, my reader, guidance in discerning with integrity and biblical faithfulness that which is closest to His divine will and Word, and in applying it to your own life and situation or that of others.

However, of one thing I feel pretty sure, and that is that the Christian Church across the world in these modern times needs to have the courage to resist and stand against the prevailing patterns of permissiveness and the tidal wave of marital breakdown. We should, in general terms, resist the notions of divorce and remarriage on any other grounds than those we have mentioned in this essay. We probably also of course need to acknowledge that we are living in a post-Christian, post-modern and sometimes neo-pagan secular society in which there will be a big gap between what the church says and what the state says. Christians being realistic probably need to allow the state to frame its own divorce laws and the best run at this by the state, as mentioned in our previous chapter, may be in terms of the notion of "irretrievable breakdown'. But the Christian church should not compromise the basic teachings and principles of our Lord Jesus Christ and pastors must bring the appropriate mix of discipline and compassion where marriages have failed, for whatever reason. Pastors will from time to time feel a freedom to advise the legitimacy of a separation without a divorce, or a divorce without a remarriage, unless the grounds for divorce are adultery or desertion. This is far more likely to be a meaningful service to society than taking the route of compromise and simply becoming a pale shadow of the world's way of thinking and behaving.

The aftermath of divorce

In continuing our reflection, we do need also to consider how and what to think if divorce has already become a reality, for whatever reason. If it has, then of course a whole new set of issues comes into play. The first of these relates to the results of divorce. Of primary concern is how the divorce affects the children.

The children

Certainly a climate of deep insecurity is created for children who are victims of their parents' divorce. This can become a permanent fact of emotional life for them. One of the parents who has been there as an emotional constant as long as the child can remember is suddenly no longer present in the home. And even where this results in an apparently better situation physically or emotionally, or when the child appears to be stoically coping, the loss of that parent is nevertheless very deeply felt, no matter how much the child pretends otherwise, or appears to be managing. Once the divorce is an accomplished fact, children often blame themselves to explain the situation, not knowing the real story. Serious false guilt becomes part of their emotional life a long time thereafter and there is ongoing suffering in many psychological and emotional ways.

Secondly, we must ask what we communicate to our children by the act of divorce. First of all, we risk teaching by attitude and example that promises and vows – about "for better or worse", "till death us do part", etc. – are not binding. The commitment we parents made to each other appears to the children to have little value as it is now to be terminated, perhaps even apparently casually terminated. The message the children receive is that there is no need to persevere when things become unpleasant or difficult. The "for better or worse" wisdom of the ages can simply be discarded. After all, we never vowed to stay together "until something-or-other us do part", but "until death us do part".

Beyond that, we note that, because the consequences of this kind of relaxed thinking about vows carry through into adult life, the proportion of "second-generation divorces" is extremely high. The fact is that the children of divorced parents often have not learned how to persevere in making a tough marriage work, their own approach to marriage perhaps having also been quite casual in the first place.

Finally, there is a fallacy which sometimes salves the conscience of couples contemplating divorce but who are concerned about its effect on their children. They affirm that a happy single-parent home is better than one in which both parents are present but in a state of tension, hostility and unhappiness. This is a precarious assumption that may not take into account the stress of raising a family single-handedly and the resentment engendered by the estrangement itself, both of which contribute to making most single-parent families less than fully satisfied and happy.

Far better, then, for the parents to move heaven and earth to find their way through to reconciliation for the sake of the children.

However, if the divorce has already happened, or is unpreventable, then some species of amicable arrangement is necessary for the partner who does not have custody of the children to have access to them on a regular basis. That is, unless abuse of the children has been a contributory cause of the marital break-up.

Another basic rule here between the parents is not to bad-mouth one another to the children in an attempt to alienate them from the other parent and win them over to their own side. Children should be spared that unconscionably awful pain.

The divorcee and remarriage

For him or her, the marriage is now gone. The decision, right or wrong, has been made. The immediate aftermath will require the divorcee to cope with deep trauma and pick up the fragments of what was once there. This can be a very consuming and complex business. With the Lord's help, however, it can be done, and often has been, praise God. As Jesus says, "Gather up the fragments left over", so there can in fact often be twelve baskets full (John 6:12-13) as our God reveals himself as Lord of the new economy, the new fullness and the second chance.

Then, of course, the question of remarriage may arise. This is another extremely delicate issue. The relevant passage is 1 Corinthians 7:10-17. Eugene Peterson, author of *The Message* Bible, translates this passage as follows:

If you are married, stay married. This is the Master's command, not mine. If a wife should leave her husband, she must either remain single or else come back and make things right with him. And a husband has no right to get rid of his wife.

For the rest of you who are in mixed marriages – Christian married to non-Christian – we have no explicit command from the Master. So this is what you must do. If you are a man with a wife who is not a believer but who still wants to live with you, hold on to her. If you are a woman with a husband who is not a believer but he wants to live with you, hold on to him. The unbelieving husband shares to an extent in the holiness of his wife, and the unbelieving wife is likewise touched by the holiness of her husband. Otherwise, your children would be left out; as it is, they also are included in the spiritual purposes of God

On the other hand, if the unbelieving spouse walks out, you've got to let him or her go. You don't have to hold on desperately. God has called us to make the best of it, as peacefully as we can. You never know, wife: The way you handle this might bring your husband not only back to you but to God. You never know, husband: The way you handle this might bring your wife not only back to you but to God.

And don't be wishing you were someplace else or with someone else. Where you are right now is God's place for you. Live and obey and love and believe right there. God, not your marital status, defines your life. Don't think I'm being harder on you than on the others. I give this same counsel in all the churches.[5]

The key passage there is verse 15, which I have italicised. The Revised Standard Version translates the vital phrase: "…in such a case the brother or sister is not bound." The New International Version says: "A believing man or woman is not bound in such circumstances."

The Greek verb used there is rooted in the word for slave (*doulos*). In other words, "she is not to feel enslaved". Robertson and Plummer, the great commentators and exegetes of yesteryear, writing in the *International Critical Commentary*, see the sense of the verse thus: "if one who remains a heathen demands divorce, the Christian is not bound to oppose divorce. In such matters the Christian … has not lost all freedom of action; independence still survives."[6]

Martin Luther interpreted this to mean that a Christian partner divorced by a non-Christian partner may marry again. And most modern exegetes would agree.

Robertson and Plummer feel that the phrase translated "not bound" or not enslaved means only "that he or she need not feel so bound by Christ's prohibition on divorce as to be afraid to depart when the heathen partner insists on separation."[6]

For Peterson, the sense is "you don't have to hold on desperately" – i.e., slavishly.

The corollary of this, most would agree, is that the innocent party is free to remarry. The key notion here, however, is that the permissibility of remarriage in Christian terms is linked to the grounds of divorce and whether they were valid or not.

What we can also say is that, while the Jews of Jesus' day may have argued about the grounds for divorce, nevertheless it was not in dispute that a divorced person could remarry. And, as best scholars can discern, Jesus would not appear to have altered this.

Many do feel on this that some concession to human fallibility and failure is needed for those considering remarriage. John Stott asserted well that "The primary question is how (the Church) may find some arrangement that will give adequate form both to its beliefs about the permanence of marriage and to its beliefs about the forgiveness of the penitent sinner. It could express its ambivalence either by permitting the remarriage in church (thereby emphasising the gospel of redemption), while adding some kind of discipline (thereby recognising God's marriage ideal), or by refusing remarriage in church (thereby emphasising the ideal), while adding some expression of acceptance (thereby recognising the gospel)."[7] He inclines to the former. The fact is that the intention of marriage and the gospel of redemption stand in tension with one another, forcing us to find a compromise between the two which expresses both the divine intention and the divine compassion for us when we fail to reach it.

Conclusion

Without question, the Jesus way for marriage does not include any easy breaking of the marital bond. In looking at what the Bible says concerning divorce, in examining the three views of how to apply the biblical text to the Christian life and community, and in taking a look at the devastating effects of divorce not only on children but on the estranged partners themselves, not to mention the community as a whole, we have sought to shed some light on this troubling issue. All of this has been with the understanding that, although divorce is always to be resisted and a stand made against it, nevertheless God's love never ceases to cover the persons involved. Moreover the Scripture promise in 1 John 1:9 concerning confession, forgiveness and cleansing covers all areas of our fallenness and frailty, including this one.

In closing, let's underline that it might be well in the modern Church to spend a whole lot more time on pre-marital teaching and moral education, even in schools, thus ensuring responsible biblical sexuality and sound marriages. This is preferable by a thousand light-years to ignoring or neglecting all that, and then having to spend our lives trying to work out how to cope with the devastating marital breakdown consequent upon our first neglect, namely our failure adequately to prepare our young people or any others for responsible marital choices and the biblical demands of marriage and family life.

End Notes

1. Andrew Cornes, *Divorce and Remarriage*
   (London: Hodder & Stoughton, 1993), 464-465.
2. Maggie Gallagher, "Why Marriage is Good for You",
   Autumn 2000, *City Journal*, <http://www.city-journal.org/html/10_
   4_why_marriage_is.html>, March 2, 2006.
3. William Barclay, *The Gospel of Matthew – Vol. 2*
   (Edinburgh: Saint Andrew Press, 1967), 230.
4. Barclay, 230-31.
5. Eugene H. Peterson, *The Message – The Bible in Contemporary Language*
   (Colorado Springs: Navpress, 2002), 2074, italics mine.
6. Archibald Robertson and Alfred Plummer, "A Critical and Exegetical
   Commentary on the First Epistle of Paul to the Corinthians", in
   *The International Critical Commentary on the Holy Scriptures of the Old
   and New Testaments*, S.R. Driver, A. Plummer and C.A. Briggs, eds.
   (Edinburgh: T. & T. Clark, 1958), 143.
7. John Stott, *Issues Facing Christians Today*
   (London: Marshall Pickering, 1990), 305.

Chapter Five

HOMOSEXUALITY – AN ISSUE FOR COMPASSION AND CONCERN IN THE CHURCH TODAY

I want now to tackle the vitally important but highly sensitive issue of homosexuality. It is an issue calling, I believe, for both great compassion and great concern in the Church of Jesus Christ today.

Right at the outset I want to register a principle which I feel is critical – namely that to express the view that homosexual practice or behaviour is not morally or biblically acceptable is not to be equated with homophobia. Homophobic responses to this issue are totally unacceptable and not in line with the biblical requirements of compassion, love and understanding.

In my own experience I have been ministered to and been blessed by homosexually oriented people who were sexually celibate and Christians of great integrity who carried out effective and significant ministries. Beyond that, I have had the privilege of ministering to practising homosexuals for whom I felt profound Christian love, compassion and acceptance. And the fact that I accepted them and believed they could be healed and come to normal heterosexuality was apparently significant to them in our pastoral encounters.

So it is against this backdrop that I share the following reflections.

Some steps to a biblical perspective

Let us begin first of all with some procedural steps alluded to in chapter one on ethics which I think are key as we try to reach a proper and biblical perspective on the present marital and sexuality situation generally, and homosexuality more specifically.

1. Accept that the Bible is the supreme authority for the Church in all matters of faith and morals.

2. Grasp by faith and demonstrate from Scripture and experience that we live in a God-created universe of physical, spiritual and moral law.
3. Grasp that if Jesus is the cosmic Christ, the agent in creation (John 1:3), and the Logos or self-expression of God, who was and is God, then the universe as His creation will have a moral fabric and a Jesus way for behaviour built into it.
4. Ascertain how the Scriptures generally – and Jesus and the apostles specifically – view the divine way for sexuality in terms of creation's plan and God's creation ordinances.
5. Emphasise to the world around us that non-Jesus ways do not work in terms of our fullest happiness, greatest fulfilment, and our maximum health.
6. Affirm and reaffirm without loss of nerve the Bible's way for sexuality, marriage, and family life.

These simple principles must guide our reflection, rather than the world's constantly vacillating verdicts on faith and behaviour.

Homosexual arguments and the biblical response

I want now to consider several arguments that have been made in order to support the notion that homosexual practice is not immoral or problematic, and then seek to offer a biblical response and counter-argument.

Argument 1

Homosexuality is genetically determined. Homosexuals are made thus by their genes and cannot change to become otherwise.

The media may say this, but most in the scientific community would not agree. One of the foremost authorities on the subject is Dr Jeffrey Satinover who has practised psychoanalysis and psychiatry for more than twenty years. He is a former Fellow in Psychiatry and Child Psychiatry at Yale University and past William James Lecturer in Psychology and Religion at Harvard University. He holds degrees from the Massachusetts Institute of Technology, Harvard and the University of Texas. He diagnosed one of the first patients in North America to contract AIDS. In his book, *Homosexuality and the Politics of Truth*, Satinover asserts that,

Recent articles in the media create the mistaken impression that scientific closure on the subject of homosexuality will be reached. Such actions as the APA's (American Psychological Association) 1973 decision and its recent deliberations further reinforce unjustified conclusions in the public mind. Few understand the complexities of good biological research; most would be amazed at the extent that politics has corrupted the scientific process. They depend on the accuracy of the accounts in the popular press.

But the purported scientific consensus that the press touts is a fiction. A good example is Chandler Burr's article in the March 1993 issue of the *Atlantic Monthly* ["Homosexuality and Biology", by C Burr, *Atlantic Monthly* 271, No. 3 March 1993, 47-65]. He states baldly: "Five decades of psychiatric evidence demonstrates that homosexuality is immutable, and non-pathological, and a growing body of more recent evidence implicates biology in the development of sexual orientation." In a later *New York Times* opinion piece he states even more flatly that science has long since proven that homosexuality is biological and unchangeable, and that *there is simply no disagreement on this among scientists.*

But *these claims are absolutely not true,* except for the meaningless statement that "biology is implicated in the development of homosexuality." Biology is, of course, "implicated" in everything human. In conducting his research for the *Atlantic Monthly,* Burr interviewed a number of scientists and clinicians who expressed the view that homosexuality is neither genetic nor immutable. He simply did not cite them.[1]

Satinover goes on to elaborate with chapter and verse of scholarly research and facts "the falsity of the activists' repeated assertions that homosexuality is immutable. They seek to create the impression that *science* has settled these questions, but it most certainly has not. Instead, the changes that have occurred in both public and professional opinion have resulted from politics, pressure, and public relations."[2]

Satinover then adds:

> In contrast to the widely promoted claims, many eminent scientists disagree with the media's conclusions about the "biology of homosexuality." A scientist who leads one of the nation's largest behavioural genetics laboratories commented that the latest genetics research only means that some tentative, indirect, partial genetic relationship *might* exist, so perhaps it is worth looking into.

> *Scientific American*'s cover read "The dubious link between genes and behaviour." But what is remembered by the general public is the catchy, inaccurate headline in a major newsweekly: "The Gay Gene."[3]

Not surprisingly then, Satinover also claims that "the sociological – not medical or scientific – transformation of the opinion of mental health professionals regarding homosexuality has greatly influenced the current research."[4] In other words, society – rather than medical and scientific professionals – is determining the conclusions of many, even some researchers.

We should at this point also register the conclusion of Dr Charles Socarides, clinical professor of psychiatry in the Albert Einstein College of Medicine in New York City. Socarides notes that "the 1973 APA decision remains a chilling reminder that if scientific principles are not fought for, they can be lost – a disillusioning warning that unless we make no exceptions to science, we are subject to the snares of political factionalism and the propagation of untruths to an unsuspecting and uninformed public, to the rest of the medical profession and to the behavioural sciences."[5]

Satinover makes another point: "Demonstrating that any behavioural state – let alone one so complex, diverse in its manifestations and nuance as homosexuality – is only biological but *genetic* is well beyond our present research capacity."[6]

Dr John Money, a sex researcher from Johns Hopkins University in the United States, has said, "No chromosomal differences have been found between homosexual subjects and heterosexual controls. [and later] On the basis of present knowledge, there is no basis on which to justify an hypothesis that homosexuals or bisexuals of any degree or type are discrepant [different] from heterosexuals."[7]

Lest it appears that this is only the opinion of anti-homosexual groups, Dr John De Cecco, a homosexual who is editor of the *Journal of Homosexuality*: "The idea that people are born into one type of sexual behaviour is foolish."[8]

One of the famous researchers on this issue is Dr Simon LeVay, who sought to prove a genetic cause for homosexuality, but failed. LeVay said of his work, as well as that of others: "At the moment it's still a very big mystery. Not even my work nor any other work that's been done so far really totally clarifies the situation of what makes people gay or straight... In fact, the twin studies, for example, suggest that it's not totally inborn because even identical twins are not always of the same sexual orientation."[9]

Masters and Johnson, in their book *Human Sexuality*, have said, "The genetic theory of homosexuality has been generally discarded today ... no serious scientists suggest that a simple cause-effect relationship exists."[10]

Still other scholars will acknowledge that, even if there is some genetic predisposition in some to homosexuality, this never overwhelms or supersedes environmental or social conditioning factors.

Suppose, however, that we were to concede the theory of genetic predisposition. In a sense my reply would be "So what?" Are not you and I, as fallen sinners, all genetically conditioned, if you like, to be adulterers, liars, deceivers, or whatever? I should think the average man, if he were honest with himself, would probably be able to say, "I am genetically conditioned to be adulterous. My instincts are polygamous. I often have unfaithful thoughts to my wife. I am genetically that way." So, even if we were genetically conditioned, it does not remove moral responsibility from our behavioural choices, or excuse either homosexual or heterosexual sin on either genetic or environmental grounds.

Argument 2

Homosexuals often claim to be 10 percent of the population. Such a significant percentage must mean that homosexuality is normal and acceptable.

This 10 percent statistic is based on the flawed evidence-gathering techniques of Alfred Kinsey, as agreed by all. Writes Thomas Schmidt in his scholarly work, *Straight and Narrow?*:

> ...the 10 percent figure was so often repeated that it gradually gained a life of its own and was until very recently assumed in most discussions of homosexuality. Numbers do not in themselves establish the

morality of an activity, but a number as large as 10 percent – the equivalent of twenty-five million Americans – seems to attach a degree of normalcy to homosexuality. Thus out of the moral fog of the last few decades, the notion emerged that 10 percent equals normal, and normal equals natural, and natural equals acceptable.

This notion is much harder to maintain in the light of more than a dozen recent studies that consistently put the incidence of homosexual practice around 1 percent."[11]

Schmidt says the number of currently active homosexuals in the States is 0.6 percent to 0.7 percent, i.e., less than 1 percent. In Britain it is established at 1.1 percent, in the Netherlands 3.3 percent of men, 0.4 percent of women.[12]

Whitehead, summarising what he calls "more than thirty surveys of homosexual incidence ... based on genuinely representative samples, mostly from Western countries"[13] presents the following conclusions:

Homosexual incidence in Western adult populations is much lower than one in ten. About 0.9 percent of adult males are exclusively homosexual and about 0.5 percent of adult women are exclusively lesbian. The figure for bisexuality and exclusive homosexuality combined rises to about 2.7 percent for males and 1.7 percent for females, an average of 2.2 percent of the total adult population. Much of the alleged bisexual component could comprise homosexuals and lesbians who are or have been married, but, even then, the figure falls far short of Kinsey's 10 percent.

Both Kinsey's figures and modern incidence surveys support a greater environmental contribution to homosexuality than a genetic one. People move away from homosexual behavior with age (meaning the condition cannot be genetically determined), the incidence is too high for homosexuality and bisexuality to sit easily in the genetic category, and even the strongest arguments in favor of genetic homosexuality still show that environmental factors are at least twice as strong in the development of homosexuality, and probably many times stronger.[14]

Argument 3
There can be nothing wrong with long-term committed monogamous and faithful same-sex unions.

First, people can only say there is nothing wrong with monogamous homosexual relationships if they choose to elevate contemporary society's current verdict above the teaching of Scripture. But we must also register the fact that same-sex unions, with very rare exceptions, are not in fact monogamous in the long term, nor even very frequently in the short term. According to Schmidt,

> ...the most thorough study of homosexual relationships to date is reported by A.P. Bell and M.S. Wynberg in their book *Homosexualities*. The authors classify as "close-coupled" the nearest approximation to marriage among homosexuals, which involves cohabiters in a "quasi-marriage" where the "amount of cruising [sexual encounters extraneous to the primary relationship] also had to be low. Only 10 percent of the male subjects and 28 percent of the female subjects were found to fit into this category.[15]

Furthermore, says Schmidt:

> We can quantify the phenomenon of homosexual promiscuity, especially among males, more specifically. The numbers are astounding. Bell and Weinberg found that 74 percent of male homosexuals reported having more than one hundred partners in their lifetime, 41 percent more than five hundred partners, 28 percent more than one thousand partners. Seventy-five percent reported that more than half their partners were strangers, and 65 percent reported that they had sex with more than half their partners only once. For the previous year, 55 percent reported twenty or more partners, 30 percent fifty or more partners.[16]

Another study, by M.T. Saghir and E. Robins, "found that 50 percent of homosexual men over the age of thirty, and 75 percent of homosexual men over the age of forty, experienced *no* relationships that lasted more than one year... And overall, only 8 percent of the homosexual men and 7 percent of the homosexual women *ever* had relationships that lasted more than three years."[17]

Schmidt writes as follows:

> If we project these numbers out over several years, the number of homosexual men who experience anything like lifelong fidelity becomes, statistically speaking, almost meaningless.

> Promiscuity among homosexual men is not a mere stereotype, and it is not merely the majority experience – it is virtually the *only* experience. And even if we set aside infidelity and allow a generous definition of "long-term relationships" as those that last at least four years,

under 8 percent of either male or female homosexual relationships fit the definition. In short, there is practically no comparison possible to heterosexual marriage in terms of either fidelity or longevity. Tragically, lifelong faithfulness is almost nonexistent in the homosexual experience.[18]

So the picture of long-term monogamous quasi-marital homosexual relationships does not register well in terms of the faithfulness factor. Its validity therefore as an argument is highly questionable. In other words, lifelong faithfulness is rare in both the homosexual and lesbian experience.

Argument 4

The Bible does not really condemn homosexuality, only unloving relationships such as rape, pederasty (the love of an adult male for a pubescent boy), promiscuity, etc. If there is condemnation, it is culturally conditioned and, even then, the interpretation of the text is from heterosexual interpreters and therefore biased and prejudiced. As for Jesus, he had nothing to say on the subject.

At this point, we must pause to reiterate some basic hermeneutical principles (i.e., principles of interpretation) relating to the Bible. Believing that God has granted us a progressive revelation in our biblical text, we should hold to the following hermeneutical principles: that the New Testament interprets the Old; the Epistles interpret the Gospels; the clear interprets the obscure; the universal interprets the local and cultural; the systematic and didactic – like Romans and Galatians – interpret the historical and incidental. Beyond that, we assert that Scripture has a basic clarity which is based on what we call the grammatico-historical method of interpretation. This method is simple. First, it asks what does the grammar, syntax and vocabulary of the verse or passage say? Second, what did it mean in the original historical context? Third, what does it mean in our context now?

When we have our hermeneutic clear, we can come to the texts of Old and New Testaments and ask, "Does the New Testament affirm and reaffirm the Old Testament text on homosexuality, or revoke and reinterpret it?" To me, it seems very clear that the New Testament affirms, reaffirms and even strengthens the

Old Testament posture of hostility to homosexual practice (e.g., Genesis 19:4-8; Leviticus 18:22ff.; 20:13; Judges 19:22-24). There are, incidentally and not surprisingly, some revisionist interpretations of these texts by homosexual sympathisers, but the vast majority of biblical exegetes from the first century to the twenty-first are agreed that these Old Testament texts constitute strong condemnation of homosexual practice. Attempts to make them do otherwise are special pleading – a case of "If the will desires the end, the reason will find the means."[19] (Further comments are found at this end note entry.)

But back now to our hermeneutic where we have to ask: "Is there a universal set of texts or principles on this subject to interpret those that might seem obscure or confusing?" Again, I believe we have to say, "Yes, there is a clear set of affirmations in Scripture on a universal norm for sexuality, rooted in creation and in the natural and divinely constituted order of things."

Creation the key concept

It is important here to register that the biblical antipathy to homosexual practice does not rest on a few isolated proof-texts whose traditional interpretation, as some claim, can be overthrown. No! It is based on the overall biblical and creational principle affirmed in Genesis and confirmed by Jesus, relating to how God has established and structured His will and purposes for human sexuality. So Genesis says, "male and female he created them" (Genesis 1:27). "Therefore a man leaves his father and his mother and cleaves to his wife, and they become one flesh" (Genesis 2:24). This is the divine plan for marriage and sexuality established as a fundamental and basic creation ordinance.

Jesus then, picking it up in the New Testament, affirms this creation ordinance by saying, "Have you not read that he who made them from the beginning made them male and female, and said, 'For this reason a man shall leave his father and mother and be joined to his wife, and the two shall become one flesh'? So they are no longer two but one flesh. What therefore God has joined together, let not man put asunder" (Matthew 19:4-6). Jesus gives no space to any other expression of human sexuality.

So, as John Stott says, seeing Jesus has made this affirmation, "no other kind of marriage or sexual intercourse" is provided for in Scripture "for God provided no other alternative."[20]

Meeting in Dallas, Texas, in September 1997, 45 Anglican bishops and four archbishops put the point this way: "A biblical theology of sexuality must reckon not merely with specific texts but with the whole biblical story, which tells of God's purposes for human life and identity from creation to new creation. It is not from isolated texts but from the consistent teaching of the whole of Scripture that lifelong heterosexual monogamy emerges as the God-given norm for sexual relationships. Scripture offers no positive examples of non-marital sex; and it contains specific condemnations of fornication and homosexual practice as sin."[21] I believe the bishops are right, this group of bishops anyway!

So, to say that Jesus said nothing about homosexuality is a two-edged sword. Because if He said nothing that explicitly and specifically condemned homosexuality, it was only because it was not necessary to do so. He simply left the Old Testament hostility to it firmly in place and He did not revoke it. He did not say more because He did not need to. So, too, Paul in Romans 1 takes this high ground of the creation ordinance and nature and the constituted order of things, and condemns homosexual practice as "exchanged natural relations [i.e., sex] for unnatural" (Greek: *para phusin*). Jude, talking about Sodom and Gomorrah, writes in verse 7 about people "giving themselves over to fornication and going after strange flesh" (KJV). But more recent translators are absolutely clear that what is referred to there is "unnatural lust" (RSV). The Amplified Bible says "unnatural vice and sexual perversity". The NIV uses the word "perversion". In other words, the basic New Testament word on homosexuality speaks about that which is against nature and contrary to the divinely created natural order.

This posture is also in line not only with all other world religions, but with twenty centuries of Christian moral theology, from the Patristics right the way through to modern times. Indeed, it is only in the last couple of decades that anybody anywhere has seriously questioned the interpretation of the Christian church over twenty centuries on this subject.

The importance of ministry to homosexuals

In the light of this, it is clear that Christians must minister with deep compassion to the homosexual, gay or lesbian person, believing that such a person can be healed. This requires us to surrender the notion of "irreversibility" or genetic predestination through "a gay gene". Gays can change. Many do. Homosexuals can be healed. Many have been.

Thus can Jeffrey Satinover tell of a light-bulb moment in his career when he went to a conference in Kansas, "not knowing what I would find."

> What I found was that about two hundred of the three hundred people in attendance were homosexuals, male and female, struggling to emerge out of their homosexuality. And among the conference leadership a large number were *former homosexuals*, some now married and with children, all devoted to helping others out of the gay lifestyle. They were remarkable, tender human beings, enviable in their humanity and humility and in their longing for a connectedness to God. From out of the cosmopolitan desert that offers itself as the best that life has to offer, I had stepped directly into an oasis with a rushing torrent – not just a well – of living water.
>
> Nothing in my experience prepared me for this ... conference.[22]

He adds that, with some homosexuals really seeking to change, there is "a very high success rate, in some instances nearing 100 percent, for groups of highly motivated" individuals.[23]

A survey of secular treatments for homosexuality revealed "an overall success rate of over 50 percent – where success is defined as 'considerable' to 'complete' change."[24] Says Satinover: "These reports clearly contradict claims that change is flatly impossible. Indeed, it would be more accurate to say that *all the existing evidence suggests strongly that homosexuality is quite changeable.*"[25] Indeed, "The record of purely secular 'treatments' for homosexuality is far better than activists and the popular press would lead us to believe."[26] Masters and Johnson reported in 1984 "a five-year follow-up success rate of 65 percent".[27]

In a postscript to his book, Satinover movingly concludes:

> I have been extraordinarily fortunate to have met many people who have emerged from the gay life. When I see the personal difficulties they have squarely faced, the sheer courage they have displayed not only in facing these difficulties but also in confronting a culture that uses every possible means to deny the validity of their values, goals, and experiences, I truly stand back in wonder. Certainly they have forced me by the simple testimony of their lives to return again and again to my own self-examination. It is these people – former homosexuals and those still struggling, all across America and abroad – who stand for me as a model of everything good and possible in a world that takes the human heart, and the God of that heart, seriously. In my various explorations within the worlds of psychoanalysis, psychotherapy, and psychiatry, I have simply *never* before seen such profound healing.[28]

Thus the testimony of a prominent New York psychiatrist.

Needless to say, there are many other testimonies of people who have been healed of these proclivities. A friend ministering for Christ in gay bars in San Francisco told me that she had first-hand experience over a couple of years of no fewer than 27 homosexuals who were healed and restored to sexual normality. In Australia and in America I have met others.

Also notable is the experience of Andrew Comiskey, already referred to, who wrote a book called *Pursuing Sexual Wholeness*. The book tells of Comiskey's own story of healing. In the foreword to the book, Leanne Payne states, "In many years of praying for and seeing the healing of men and women who suffer with gender inferiority and confusion, I have been rendered almost incredulous at times to see how quickly these people can mature into strong Christians – even creative leaders in the body of Christ. Andy Comiskey is a prime example... When people suffering severe gender confusion find healing, it's evident to everyone."[29]

Indeed, Comiskey asserts that

> Homosexual strugglers *can* change. But they cannot accomplish the transition alone. A purely self-motivated effort will fail because of the deep and powerful roots of sexual identity. Change occurs only, however, slowly, as they submit the struggle to their Creator and

Redeemer, as well as to trusted others who stand with them in the process of becoming whole.

That process is my own. I stand in awe of my heavenly Father's capacity to effect change and to uphold me in His love along the way. This journey from a homosexual to a heterosexual identity has been revelatory. It has shown God's heart toward me: a compassion faithful enough to abide with me, even in darkness, and powerful enough to expose the darkness and awaken the weak, unaffirmed areas within.[30]

Conclusion

In closing, let me quote from a statement similar to the one already mentioned from the Anglican meeting in Dallas. This came out of another Anglican conference held in Kuala Lumpur, Malaysia, in February 1997. The eighty delegates represented the Anglican churches in the entire southern hemisphere, which contain between 80 percent and 90 percent of all Anglicans worldwide. The statement was unanimously endorsed and said that "The Scripture bears witness to God's will regarding human sexuality which is to be expressed only within the life long union of a man and a woman in (holy) matrimony."[31]

The statement mentions later the deep concern of the delegates over "the setting aside of biblical teaching in such actions as the ordination of practicing homosexuals and the blessing of same-sex unions."[32] In other words, this whole issue is more about Scripture than about sex and is therefore a watershed issue. Thankfully, when many of these same Bishops were meeting with all other Bishops of the Anglican Church at their Lambeth Conference in 1998, there was a landslide vote (641 to 70, with 45 abstentions) declaring homosexual practice unacceptable from a biblical point of view.

This is how the relevant sections of the Lambeth Conference Resolution read:

This Conference: ...

(b) in view of the teaching of Scripture, upholds faithfulness in marriage between a man and a woman in lifelong union, and believes that abstinence is right for those who are not called to marriage;

(c) recognises that there are among us persons who experience themselves as having a homosexual orientation. Many of these are members of the Church and are seeking the pastoral care, moral direction of the Church, and God's transforming power for the living of their lives and the ordering of relationships. We commit ourselves to listen to the experience of homosexual persons and we wish to assure them that they are loved by God and that all baptised, believing and faithful persons, regardless of sexual orientation, are full members of the Body of Christ;

(d) while rejecting homosexual practice as incompatible with Scripture, calls on all our people to minister pastorally and sensitively to all irrespective of sexual orientation and to condemn irrational fear of homosexuals, violence within marriage and any trivialisation and commercialisation of sex;

(e) cannot advise the legitimising or blessing of same sex unions nor ordaining those involved in same gender unions;[33]

Notwithstanding some dissenting voices in both Anglican and other major denominations, these statements from Dallas, Kuala Lumpur and Lambeth, as well as innumerable other voices that have spoken out from both Church and scientific circles, further convince me, and profoundly so, that the line taken on this subject in this chapter is biblically faithful and right. It represents, I believe, the one most in tune not only with Jesus, nature, human physiology, creation and Scripture, but with twenty centuries of Christian moral theology, together with the verdict of the vast majority of Christians worldwide today, plus all major religions on Planet Earth.

Nevertheless, we reiterate the importance of deep compassion, care and concern for those who have become caught in homosexuality or other types of gender confusion. Others of us are caught in other things. Thankfully the ground at the foot of the Cross is level for all.

End Notes

1. Jeffrey Satinover, *Homosexuality and the Politics of Truth* (Grand Rapids, Michigan: Baker Books, 1997), 37-38, italics his. The Hon. Robert Dornan read into the Congressional Record of the United States Congress his conviction that "...this is about the best book on homosexuality written in our lifetime. It should be read from sea to shining sea."

2. Satinover, 38, italics his.

3. Satinover, 38-39, italics his.

4. Satinover, 39.

5. Cited in C.W. Socarides, "Sexual Politics and Scientific Logic: The Issue of Homosexuality", *The Journal of Psychohistory* 10, No. 3 (1992), 308, quoted in Satinover, 39.

6. Satinover, 76, italics his.

7. Judd Manner, ed., *Homosexual Behavior: A modern reappraisal* (New York: Basic Books, 1980) 9, 66, quoted in John F. Ankerberg, "What 'Causes' Homosexuality? – Part 2", Ankerberg Theological Research Institute, <http://www.ankerberg.com/Articles/_PDFArchives/streams-of-life/SL2W0803.pdf>, March 8, 2006.

8. Kim Painter, "A biological theory for sexual preference", *USA Today*, March 1, 1989, pg 04 D, quoted in Ankerberg, "What 'Causes' Homosexuality? – Part 2."

9. Dr. Simon LeVay, taped interview for "The John Ankerberg Show", quoted in Ankerberg, "What 'Causes' Homosexuality? – Part 2."

10. William Masters, V.E. Johnson, R.C. Kolodny, *Human Sexuality* (Boston: Little, Brown and Company, 1984), 319-320, quoted in Ankerberg, "What 'Causes' Homosexuality? – Part 2."

11. Thomas Schmidt, *Straight and Narrow?* (Leicester, England: Inter-Varsity Press, 1995) 102.

12. Schmidt, 103-104. Schmidt elaborates his point as follows on pages 103-104 (italics his):

    A 1986–1987 study of 36,741 American adolescents found that 1 percent had had homosexual experience in the previous year (1.6 percent boys, 0.9 percent girls), and the number reporting a homosexual orientation was 0.7 percent for boys (plus 0.8 percent bisexual) and 0.2 percent for girls (plus 0.9 percent bisexual). A 1988 study of 1,880 fifteen- to nineteen-year-old males found that 0.3 percent had homosexual intercourse in the past year (1.4 percent ever), and 0.5 percent reported a homosexual orientation (plus 1 percent bisexual).

Interestingly, these numbers are consistent with data from other Western countries. A British survey conducted in 1990–1991 (among 19,000 men) found that 1.1 percent had homosexual partners in the previous year (3.6 percent ever). In the Netherlands, widely regarded as socially more liberal than most Western countries, a 1989 study (1,000 subjects) revealed 3.3 percent of men and 0.4 percent of women who declared a predominantly homosexual *preference* during the previous year (12 percent men/4 percent women ever). A 1992 French study reported 1.1 percent of men and 0.3 percent of women having had same-sex relations in the previous year, 1.4 percent/0.4 percent in the previous five years, and 4.1 percent/2.6 percent ever.

These recent studies contain controls for bias in evidence gathering and reporting. Researchers work to ensure random samples, neutral questions and interview techniques, and anonymity for participants. They adjust results to take into account occasional refusals to answer questions or to answer truthfully. This degree of care, coupled with the remarkable uniformity of the resulting numbers, brings a fair degree of certainty to the question of prevalence.

13. Neil and Briar Whitehead, *My Genes Made Me Do It!: A scientific look at sexual orientation* (Lafayette, Louisiania: Huntington House Publishers, 1999), 36.

14. Whitehead, 44-45.

15. Schmidt, 105-106. Also note Schmidt, 105-108. Satinover confirms these figures in *Homosexuality and the Politics of Truth*, 53-54.

16. Schmidt, 106.

17. Schmidt, 106-107, italics his.

18. Schmidt, 107-108, italics his. See also Satinover, 54-57.

19. A good handling of these revisionist interpretations can be found in chapter five of Schmidt (86-99). Summarising his treatment of these interpretations, Schmidt writes on page 99:

…the Bible views same-sex relations as a violation of the created good of marital union between male and female. A variety of practices and motivations for same-sex relations are evident in the biblical texts, including rape, prostitution, pederasty and relationships of mutual consent. Some references are more general and may apply to different practices. Revisionist attempts to isolate each text and show its dissimilarity to modern practice fail both because some texts defy such limitations and because details of practices and motivations miss the point.

The point is simple, and it runs like a red thread through all the passages discussed in the last two chapters. The point is marriage. When any same-sex act – with angels, with prostitutes, with boys, with mutually consenting adults – is evaluated in relation to the marital union of male and female, it falls short of the plan of God present from creation.

A further fine treatment of revisionist interpretations of both Old Testament and New Testament texts is in John Stott's chapter on "Homosexual Partnerships?" in *Issues Facing Christians Today* (London: Marshall Pickering, 1984), 336-343. The entire chapter in fact is very helpful.

20. John Stott, *Issues Facing Christians Today* (London: Marshall Pickering, 1984), 346.

21. "The Dallas Statement", The Anglican Life and Witness Conference, Dallas, Texas, September 24, 1997, <http://www.episcopalian.org/cclec/paper-dallas.htm>, March 8, 2006.

22. Satinover, 26.

23. Satinover, 51.

24. Satinover, 186.

25. Satinover, 186, italics his.

26. Satinover, 179.

27. Satinover, 187.

28. Satinover, 249, italics his.

29. Leanne Payne, from the Foreword to Andrew Comiskey, *Pursuing Sexual Wholeness: How Jesus heals the homosexual* (Lake Mary, Florida: Charisma House, 1989), 9-10.

30. Comiskey, 13, italics his.

31. "The Kuala Lumpur Statement on Human Sexuality – 2nd Encounter in the South", 10 to 15 Feb 97, Global South Anglican, <http://www.globalsouthanglican.org/index.php/weblog/comments/the_kuala_lumpur_statement_on_human_sexuality_2nd_encounter_in_the_south_10/>, March 8, 2006.

32. "The Kuala Lumpur Statement on Human Sexuality – 2nd Encounter in the South"

33. Lambeth Conference 1998 – Section I Resolutions, <http://www.anglicancommunion.org/lambeth/1/sect1rpt.html>, March 8, 2006.

Chapter Six

SAME-SEX MARRIAGE

In recent times, I have been involved in launching and helping as Co-Patron to lead the Marriage Alliance of South Africa, an organisation with the support of over 70 Christian denominations and groups, representing some 20 million South African Christians, which has been formed to seek to keep marriage heterosexual in our country and to strengthen family life. On May 17, 2005, our Constitutional Court heard an appeal brought before it by the Government of South Africa, the Marriage Alliance of South Africa and Doctors for Life. At issue was whether it is unconstitutional or not to deny so-called "marriage" to same-sex couples. On December 1, 2005, the Constitutional Court ruled that it is indeed unconstitutional to deny same-sex couples the right to marry and gave the South African parliament one year to remedy our Marriage Act accordingly.

I imagine some 98 percent of South Africans believe we should say no to same-sex marriage. Although there are some divergent views in a few mainline Protestant denominations, the vast majority of Christendom – Roman Catholic, Protestant, Anglican, Reformed, Eastern Orthodox, Coptic, and Pentecostal – is clear on this issue, as are all major world religions.

Nor is this negative response to be labelled homophobic, hetero-sexist, hetero-normative, right-wing, intolerant or fundamentalist. Such labelling is not an argument, nor an appropriate way to respond, as it risks both raising temperatures and shutting down serious and considered debate on a matter so critical. Nor should those prosecuting this debate from this author's kind of perspective ever forget the proper respect, human dignity, sensitivity and Christian love to be accorded the gay or homosexual person, as indeed any other. Debating an issue is not to deny any human's value, or sacro-sanctity under God.

Background

The background to all this in South Africa was a High Court case in which a lesbian couple sought Constitutional sanction for same-sex marriage. Their case was lost in the High Court, but then won in a ruling on November 30, 2004, in the Supreme Court of Appeal. This led the Council of the South African Christian Leadership Assembly (SACLA) – which met with 4000 Christian participants in Pretoria in July 2003 – to make representation to the Presidency and the Minister of Home Affairs. In consequence of this, and other representations no doubt, the South African Government put this on appeal. In early 2005, the Government was joined in this appeal by the newly formed Marriage Alliance of South Africa as client and *amicus curiae* ("friend of the court"). Patrons of the Marriage Alliance are Cardinal Wilfrid Napier of the Roman Catholic Church, Rev. Moss Ntlha, General Secretary of The Evangelical Alliance of South Africa and Co-Chairperson of SACLA, and myself, as Co-Chairperson of SACLA and International Team Leader of African Enterprise.

Reason for opposition

The reason for our opposition is that, in our view, so-called same-sex marriage goes against the historic heterosexual understanding of marriage recognised from creation and time immemorial. This understanding, which is prior to both law and the state, affirms marriage firstly as a given in human creation, secondly as the God-given locus of covenanted male-female bonding, sexual intimacy and mutual support, thirdly as the God-given means of procreating the human race, and finally as the best and safest God-given context for raising and nurturing children. Marriage thus has a unique socio-sexual ecology in bridging the male-female divide, managing the procreative process, establishing parental obligations to children, supporting the birthright of children to be connected to both mother and father, and connecting responsibly to society and its needs.

A creation ordinance

We must also register that no law, state or church invented marriage. They have only recognised it as a pre-existing creation ordinance rooted in biological, physiological and social realities. Governments therefore only put laws around it to protect that which they recognised as the foundational institution of human society and its civic glue, recognised by all religions, all ethnic groups, all ages and all social sectors. Remove or weaken that glue – or, put differently, cut the main threads from which our social fabric is woven – and societal stability is imperilled. As in South Africa, most constitutions never defined marriage because they did not need to. Its heterosexual and, in most Western states, its monogamous nature were assumed.[1]

Law and state limits in civil society

Because the law never gave or created marriage in the first place, it cannot now change or redefine it as same-sex marriage advocates require. That would involve a state invasion of civil society, as those organisations, religious groupings, churches, clubs, associations, friendships and loves that are properly outside the formal regulation of the state.

The point is that the state and its organs have to know their proper limits and parameters. And these can most readily be registered in the case of marriage when it is grasped that marriage is not "state-created" but rooted with our creation in maleness and femaleness. As a biological "given" therefore, it can no more be redefined to be same-sex than women can be redefined to join a "brotherhood" or men be redefined to join a "sisterhood" or boys redefined to enter a girls' high school. Why? Because a brotherhood by essence and definition is male, a sisterhood by essence and definition is female and a girls' high school is self-definitionally for girls and not boys! Likewise marriage by essence and definition is male-female so that to talk of same-sex marriage is to use an oxymoron (i.e., a contradiction in terms). It makes no sense. It's like talking about a liquid tree or boiling ice, or a four-wheeled whale. The notions are *non sequiturs*. This is exchanging marriage as it has always been known for marriage as it has never been known.

Democratic will

But if in a free society there *are* those who do want to attempt to change such a definition into something nonsensical and adjust that ageless recognition of an institution affecting every last person in a nation, or on earth for that matter, then all must know it cannot be lightly done, and certainly in a democratic state should not be done at all by a handful of unelected legal officials. That is to place too great and inappropriate a responsibility on too few. The whole nation, along with its legislature, must be democratically involved in the debate. Certainly an electoral mandate, driven by democratic demand, should be required before any such radical and massive deconstruction of traditional marriage be sanctioned. This is because marriage is not just a private affair, but a public one. So in one sense it is unfair to ask any panel of judges, who are there by state appointment and not public election, to rule alone on this very public matter. Otherwise we invite judicial encroachment on legislative authority and the democratic will and we permit judicial action to replace democracy under the guise of constitutional interpretation. Although honouring the role of the judiciary, we should not in our own societies go overboard in reallocating authority from those who have their positions by election to those who have them by appointment and who become immune to democratic review or censure by the people. The reality is that, as legislative power can be abused and need checking, so can judicial power be abused and need checking.

Of course one recognises that the majoritarian argument cannot be pushed too far, as high courts and constitutional courts must also protect minority interests. Even so, it remains true that common law in any country should normally affect the core values of that society, and same-sex marriage is not a core value in any country I know.

Integrity questionable

Beyond that, one has to challenge the integrity of this process, in so far as it is a known and conscious strategy of the gay lobby, as openly declared in many forums, that their intentions are to "bypass each nation's democratic process" and use the judicial process to secure sanctions for same-sex marriage. "Work the courts", said Evan Wolfson, former president of the Lambda Legal Defense and Educational Fund, an American gay advocacy group, "to achieve legal breakthrough. This won't be just a change in law either; it will be a change in society."[2] He spoke truly.

Erwin Lutzer, in his fine book, *The Truth about Same-Sex Marriage*, tells about "A conference at the University of London called 'Legal Recognition of Same-Sex Marriage: A Conference on National European and International Law' [which] explored the question of whether marriage should exist at all. They discussed strategies on how to bypass each nation's democratic process and use the judicial process to sanction same-sex marriages. They also discussed how adults could be free to pursue any sexual relationship they want, with no legal restrictions whatsoever."[3]

Change in marriage

Nor should we be under any illusion that a radical redefinition on same-sex marriage lines will not involve a major change in marriage itself. The fact is that the previous and ageless marriage category will have been obliterated and replaced by a new norm requiring full social sanction even if it contradicts the convictions and consciences of the vast majority of the populace. That's why it's not a case of live and let live. It's not like adding oil to a glass of water where the two coexist. It's like adding drops of raspberry colouring which changes the whole complexion of the water. It's like a few passengers on a boat drilling a hole in it and saying it won't affect the other passengers. In reality the hole will affect everyone because all are thereby imperilled.

This is because the marital redefinition we are asked to sanction is radical, and without precedent in all human history – until recently in a few Western countries – and requires social sanction from multitudes whose religious convictions and consciences do not allow them to give it. This means it is also profoundly divisive in a society.

Place of belief

One should also note in terms of the legal process that it is inappropriate for legal officials to rule out the beliefs of a religious majority on the ground that we live in "a secular state", as if those same judges had no belief systems themselves. Every person in fact is a "believer" with faith assumptions in something or someone (even if agnostic, atheist or secularist). The question is: which faith assumptions are to prevail when social decisions are made? The peril is for *explicit* and religiously rooted faith claims to be discarded or put out of bounds in the name of "secularism", while *implicit* and so-called "secularist" faith assumptions rule the roost, thereby tilting the public sphere in the direction of atheism, agnosticism, secularism, or whatever, according to the various "beliefs" of the judges involved.

Secularism

Likewise, one could ask of the "secularist" state or courts for that matter how, in the name of "secular neutrality" or by what rule of moral analysis, can consciences informed by religious conviction (for example, about the nature of marriage) be overridden by consciences informed by secularist or agnostic assumptions.

What this does finally is to marginalise *explicit* religious convictions in the social and legal spheres which are then left to be dominated by so-called "non-religious" and *implicit* secularist convictions. And this even in countries like South Africa, where theism, as against atheism, predominates within the overwhelming majority.

Interestingly enough, while "secularism" was an eighteenth-century Enlightenment intellectual venture in reconstructing the world along material lines and eliminating the metaphysical and transcendent, the word "secular" is being revisited these days. Originally meaning in Latin the realm of time rather than eternity and the arena of the world rather than that which was beyond the world, the word "secular" was indeed revisited in the Canadian Supreme Court in 2002 where it was ruled – by nine judges to nil – to be not exclusive but inclusive of religion. In other words, the secular is not to be regarded as a non-sacred realm. It is just the realm of the world, but nevertheless a realm where the divine is all-pervasive, because it originates in the divine and transcendent.[4]

This means that the law cannot be applied in a way where the transcendent and metaphysical are ignored or discarded. Put differently, the legal processes of a country are not an arena where it is either obligatory or appropriate in the name of the secular for the law or its courts to ignore the religious convictions of the populace or discount either the explicit or implicit "faith assumptions" of the judges themselves. The same applies to politicians.

This is why the same-sex marriage issue is not just about marriage, but about religious freedom and the place of religion and the state in civil society.

Marriage damage

We must also note that if marriage is indeed "redefined" in a country's courts or even its parliament, the effects will be catastrophic in the long term, in that the church and all those who oppose same-sex marriage on the grounds of conscience or religious convictions will now be placed outside the new constitutional norm. The fact is that gay marriage creates a new form of legal sexual coupling which, instead of simply extending marital rights will, by state definition, abolish the understanding of traditional marriage and put a new, profoundly flawed and deeply damaged institution in its place.

This is why many pastors and even sociologists in Scandinavia, where virtual same-sex marriage has been legalised, will testify that same-sex marriage has dealt a body-blow to all of marriage. Writes Stanley Kurtz, a former research fellow at the Hoover Institution at Stanford University in California:

> Marriage is slowly dying in Scandinavia. A majority of children in Sweden and Norway are born out of wedlock. Sixty percent of first-born children in Denmark have unmarried parents. Not coincidentally, these countries have had something close to full gay marriage for a decade or more. Same-sex marriage has locked in and reinforced an existing Scandinavian trend toward the separation of marriage and parenthood. The Nordic family pattern – including

gay marriage – is spreading across Europe. And by looking closely at it we can answer the key empirical question underlying the gay marriage debate. Will same-sex marriage undermine the institution of marriage? It already has.

More precisely, it has *further* undermined the institution. The separation of marriage from parenthood was increasing; gay marriage has widened the separation. Out-of-wedlock birthrates were rising; gay marriage has added to the factors pushing those rates higher. Instead of encouraging a society-wide return to marriage, Scandinavian gay marriage has driven home the message that marriage itself is outdated, and that virtually any family form, including out-of-wedlock parenthood, is acceptable.[5]

Commenting on Norway and how gay marriage was imposed against the public will by the political elite, Kurtz notes:

Norway's gay marriage debate, which ran most intensely from 1991 through 1993, was a culture-shifting event. And once enacted, gay marriage had a decidedly unconservative impact on Norway's cultural contests, weakening marriage's defenders, and placing a weapon in the hands of those who sought to replace marriage with cohabitation. Since its adoption, gay marriage has brought division and decline to Norway's Lutheran Church. Meanwhile, Norway's fast-rising out-of-wedlock birthrate has shot past Denmark's. Particularly in Norway – once relatively conservative – gay marriage has undermined marriage's institutional standing for everyone.[6]

Beyond that, he says:

Gay marriage has given ammunition to those who would put an end to marriage.[7]

One Norwegian social scientist, speaking in favour of gay marriage, said she treated its creation "as a (welcome) death knell for marriage itself." She said that in recognising same-sex marriage "society was ratifying the division of marriage from parenthood" and she welcomed those "social pioneers forging relationships unencumbered by children."[8] This sort of thing is also why so many in Canada are now having second thoughts about what they have been rushed into.

Stanley Kurtz also observes that

Marriage in the Netherlands is in serious trouble. You don't have to take my word for it, because even the Netherlands' own statistical agency is making the same point. ... Jan Latten of the Dutch Central

Bureau of Statistics paints a picture of radical institutional decline. ...all signs point to same-sex marriage as a significant causal factor in Dutch marital decline.[9]

Kurtz says that,

Until 1997, when the Netherlands legalized Registered Partnerships, the Dutch out-of-wedlock birthrate was notably low. After 1997, the rate of non-marital births began to accelerate twice as quickly as it had been. This accelerated increase in the out-of-wedlock birthrate has continued now for eight straight years, outstripping the pace of growth in any other Western European country during the same period."

Kurtz quotes Jan Latten as writing: "Today, 40 percent of all firstborn children are born out of wedlock. Marriage is fast losing its status as the essential *sine qua non* condition of parenthood." Kurtz concludes by asking:

Why would a country with a notably traditional attitude toward marriage and parenthood all of a sudden experience such a remarkable and long-lasting spike in its out-of-wedlock birthrate? The answer is that, once marriage stops being about binding mothers and fathers together for the sake of their children, the need to get married gradually disappears. That's why I've argued that the soaring Dutch out-of-wedlock birthrate has everything to do with gay marriage.[10]

As we in South Africa look to a future that could likely include same-sex marriage, we could learn a lot from the Scandinavian countries, which have now had more than a decade's experience with this set-up. Kurtz continues:

Since liberalizing divorce in the first decades of the twentieth century, the Nordic countries have been the leading edge of marital change. Drawing on the Swedish experience, Kathleen Kiernan, the British demographer, uses a four-stage model by which to gauge a country's movement toward Swedish levels of out-of-wedlock births. In stage one, cohabitation is seen as a deviant or avant-garde practice, and the vast majority of the population produces children within marriage. Italy is at this first stage. In the second stage, cohabitation serves as a testing period before marriage, and is generally a childless phase. Bracketing the problem of underclass single parenthood, America is largely at this second stage. In stage three, cohabitation becomes increasingly acceptable, and parenting is no longer automatically associated with marriage. Norway was at this third stage, but with recent demographic and legal changes has entered stage four. In the fourth stage (Sweden and Denmark), marriage and cohabitation become practically indistinguishable, with many, perhaps even most, children born and raised outside of marriage. According to Kiernan, these stages may vary in duration, yet once a country has reached a stage, return to an earlier phase is unlikely. (She offers no examples of stage reversal.) Yet once a stage has been reached, earlier phases coexist.[11]

Children affected

Children are also profoundly affected in the long run by same-sex marriage. In reality, same-sex marriage opens up a giant experiment in social engineering at the expense of the well-being of children. Apart from anything else it denies the fundamental and foundational right and psychological need of children to have *both* a mum and a dad, unless an exception can justify this as in the child's best interests. The fact is that same-sex marriage severs children from the protections of traditional marriage and allows something which at best should be highly exceptional to become acceptable as part of a new state norm. And adult needs are inappropriately given priority over those of children as the most vulnerable in our society. The point is that non-traditional families should not be seen as within some new norm but as an exception to the traditional norm. Thus would adult rights wrongly trump those of children. It is wrong for lesbian "marriages" to legitimise the notion that fathers are unnecessary or for male couples to invalidate the necessity of a mother. Children's rights must never be made secondary to those of adults. Above all, the state, whether by its courts or legislature, should never facilitate the creation and legitimising of situations not in the best interests of children.

Wrote G.K. Chesterton: "This triangle of truisms of father, mother and child cannot be destroyed: it can only destroy those civilisations which disregard it."[12]

Margaret Somerville, professor of law and medicine at McGill University in Toronto, writes of the reasons for opposing same-sex marriage, saying:

My reasons go to the belief that children need and have a right to both a mother and father and (unless some other arrangement can be justified as in the best interests of a particular child) a right to know and be reared by their own biological parents. Restricting marriage to the union of a man and a woman establishes that right of children as the societal norm. In other words, it is a fundamental purpose of marriage to give children both a mother and a father, preferably their own biological parents. Changing the definition of marriage to include same-sex couples would overtly and directly contravene both the right and the norm and would mean marriage could no longer function to affirm the biological bond between parents and their children.

In short, marriage, as it stands, is the societal institution that represents, symbolizes, and protects the inherently reproductive human relationship for the sake of children born of such relationships. Society needs such an institution and marriage is unique in this regard; there is no other alternative.[13]

Rights and discrimination

Moreover, if marriage is no longer a union of one man and one woman, but any two persons who wish to cohabit, what or who is to say, especially if the language of rights is used, why it must be limited to two people? Why not triumvirates (two women and a man, or two men and one woman) or polyamoury (multiple partners of both sexes in a so-called marital arrangement)? And if its just rights, uncontrolled by moral principle, why not exercise a right to marry a child, or one's daughter, mother or sister?

The fact is that rights have to be exercised within some moral parameters and within certain limits of appropriateness.

This is also why confining marriage to heterosexual categories is not unfair discrimination against gays. The reality is that marriage has always had certain properly discriminatory and differentiating boundaries of appropriateness around it, as for example prohibiting a man from marrying his mother, or sister, or daughter, or someone already married, or a woman from marrying a young boy. Forbidding marriage to people of the same sex is likewise a valid, important and appropriate discriminatory procedure. It is not an unfair denial of rights.

In reality, gay rights should be studiously protected under general human rights, rather than in a special category. Moreover, rights have to intersect both with moral principle and with other rights. When sick, I have no right to insist on being in the ladies' ward in the hospital because this violates both the definitional right of the hospital to establish a ladies' ward, as well as the ladies' rights to privacy! A man has no right saying he must enter a nunnery. A woman may not enter a brotherhood. Nothing unfair about that. No rights infringed there.

So a self-definitionally heterosexual institution since creation is not "unfairly discriminating" nor infringing on anyone's rights in disallowing same-sex marriage. It is nevertheless essential to oppose homophobia and accord gay people the social understanding and loving acceptance rightfully due to any human being. But no rights are being infringed to disallow them the heterosexual category of marriage.

Furthermore, it is apparent from the Scandinavian experience that relatively very few gays actually want to get married. Stanley Kurtz says that "Take-up rates on gay marriage are exceedingly small. Yale [University]'s William Eskridge [a gay marriage advocate] acknowledged this when he reported in 2000 that 2,372 couples had registered after nine years of the Danish law, 674 after four years of the Norwegian law, and 749 after four years of the Swedish law."[14]

Pandora's box

In this regard, countries contemplating legalising same-sex marriage must register that, unless these sorts of moral boundaries and social limits of appropriateness are maintained, the opening Pandora's box will make the sexual revolution of the 1960s and '70s look like a Sunday school outing. Once these wheels are set in motion, the road to a dark and dysfunctional marital future is embarked upon. And even heterosexual marriage, which is already under considerable duress in our morally and religiously confused society, will be perilously put under further pressure.

Indeed, Daniel R. Heimbach, professor of Christian ethics at Southeastern Baptist Theological Seminary in North Carolina, has written of the research undertaken

> In the early twentieth century, the British social scientist J.D. Unwin conducted a massive study of 6 major civilizations and 80 lesser

societies covering 5,000 years of history in order to understand how sexual behavior affects the rise and fall of social groups. ...He set out expecting to find evidence supporting Sigmund Freud's theory that civilizations are essentially neurotic and destroy themselves by restricting sex too much. But to Unwin's surprise, all the evidence he discovered pointed exactly the other way.[15]

According to Heimbach,

Unwin found, without exception, that if a social group limited sex to marriage, and especially to lifelong monogamous marriage, it would always prosper. There was "no recorded case of a society adopting absolute monogamy without displaying expansive energy." ...In contrast, if a social group lowered standards so that sex was no longer limited to marriage, it always lost social energy.[16]

Concluded Unwin:

In human records there is no instance of a society retaining its energy after a complete new generation has inherited a tradition which does not insist on pre-nuptial (premarital) and post-nuptial (extramarital) continence (i.e., faithfulness).[17]

Unwin was not the only social scientist to come to these conclusions. "The eminent Harvard sociologist, Pitirim Sorokin, analysed cultures spanning several thousand years on several continents, and found that virtually no society has ceased to regulate sexuality within marriage as defined as the union of a man and a woman, and survived."[18]

In light of this, it is crucial to note the effects that not only same-sex marriage will have on society, but that it will doubtlessly open the door to revive and encourage polygamy. For when you have said that it doesn't matter whether a man and a woman comprise a marriage, or two men or two women, then on what logical and moral basis do you say that polygamy is not acceptable? In fact, historically polygamy would have a greater claim to legitimacy than would same-sex marriage, since it has been practised from ancient times up even to the present in some cultures.

There are, in fact, moves afoot even now in the West to legalise polygamy. Says Stanley Kurtz: "In mid-January [2006], Canada was rocked by news that a Justice Department study had called for the decriminalization and regulation of polygamy." But, he says, the "Canadian public cannot bring itself to believe that the abolition of marriage is the real agenda of the country's liberal legal-political elite." This is because those advocating for both same-sex marriage and polygamy use what Kurtz calls "a semi-incomprehensible intellectual gibberish, with the really scary stuff hidden in footnotes." In Canada, they are also appealing to the rights of the small Mormon and Muslim populations in the drive for polygamy. But the "way to abolish marriage, without seeming to abolish it", which is the real aim of the Canadian liberal legal-political elite, "is to redefine the institution out of existence. If everything can be marriage, pretty soon nothing will be marriage. Legalize gay marriage, followed by multi-partner marriage, and pretty soon the whole idea of marriage will be meaningless. At that point, Canada can move to ... an infinitely flexible relationship system that validates any conceivable family arrangement, regardless of the number or gender of partners." "Canada", says Kurtz, "is a whole lot closer to abolishing marriage than you realize."[19]

But polygamy is not the only practice that will ensue once same-sex marriage is legalised. Polyamoury is the new buzzword among social theorists, and is a practise which features multiple loves all within one relational or marital set-up. In fact, Stanley Kurtz highlights one such example, again from the Netherlands, where a 46-year-old man, Victor de Bruijn, and his 31-year-old wife of eight years, Bianca, enacted a "cohabitation contract" with "Mirjam Geven, a recently divorced 35-year-old whom they'd met several years previously through an Internet chatroom." Says Kurtz:

> When Mirjam Geven first met Victor and Bianca de Bruijn, she was married. Yet after several meetings between Mirjam, her then-husband, and the De Bruijns, Mirjam left her spouse and moved in with Victor and Bianca. The threesome bought a bigger bed, while Mirjam and her husband divorced. Although neither Mirjam nor Bianca had had a prior relationship with a woman, each had believed for years that she was bisexual. Victor, who describes himself as "100 percent heterosexual", attributes the trio's success to his wives' bisexuality, which he says has the effect of preventing jealousy.[20]

In polygamy, a man has multiple wives with whom he engages in sexual relations, but the wives do not relate to one another in sexual intimacy.[21] Or, in much rarer instances, a woman would have several husbands with whom she engages sexually, but the husbands do not relate sexually. But in polyamoury, there can be several partners in various combinations of male and female, some or all of whom have sexual relations with one another and the set-up features heterosexuality, bisexuality and homosexuality. While the above example from the Netherlands was not, strictly speaking, marriage, it was a legally recognised relationship in a country that had already legalised same-sex marriage. Unless proper moral and social brakes are applied, it can only be a matter of time before polyamorous partners gain the right to full-fledged marriage.

Another aim of some gay activists is to pave the way for legalised paedophilia. Says the LifeSite in Canada: "Homosexual activists have long sought to distance themselves from pedophiles, however Canada's most prominent homosexual activist group has now demanded the lowering the age of consent for anal sex to 16 from 18."[22] Daniel Heimbach has written that, "Out of seven principal demands listed in the platform published for the 1993 March on Washington for Lesbian, Gay, and Bi Equal Rights, five were specifically aimed at altering the fundamental structure of family relationships. Number one called for legalizing any sort of 'non-coercive' sexual behavior between adults' and replacing age-of-consent laws with more lenient 'graduated age-of-consent laws.'"[23]

The potential threats to marriage don't end there, however. To quote Kurtz again:

> Ironically, the form of gay matrimony that may pose the greatest threat to the institution of marriage involves heterosexuals. A Brigham Young University professor, Alan J. Hawkins, suggests an all-too-likely scenario in which two heterosexuals of the same sex might marry as a way of obtaining financial benefits. Consider the plight of an underemployed and uninsured single mother in her early 30s who sees little real prospect of marriage (to a man) in her future. Suppose she has a good friend, also female and heterosexual, who is single and childless but employed with good spousal benefits. Sooner or later,

friends like this are going to start contracting same-sex marriages of convenience. The single mom will get medical and governmental benefits, will share her friend's paycheck, and will gain an additional caretaker for the kids besides. Her friend will gain companionship and a family life. The marriage would obviously be sexually open. And if lightning struck and the right man came along for one of the women, they could always divorce and marry heterosexually.[24]

Professor Hawkins' conclusion is that such arrangements "would turn marriage into the moral equivalent of a Social Security benefit."[25]

Continuing attack

We should note that the attack on traditional family marriage will surely escalate. Professor Pierre de Vos, of Cape Town's University of the Western Cape Faculty of Law, in calling for people to move away from heterosexuality as "the normative basis for policy formulation", writes that those institutions which maintain this must be put "under attack". Adds De Vos, "a prime candidate for reinvention or reconstruction must surely be the institutions of 'marriage' or 'the family'."[26]

Indeed, the hostility towards the institution of marriage on the part of some gay activists, feminists and other social engineers is truly alarming. Their aim is to deconstruct marriage, bit by bit, until it no longer exists, thereby "freeing" people to engage in whatever sorts of sexual relationships of whatever number of people and whatever duration they like. Daniel Heimbach has gathered numbers of disturbing quotes from marriage deconstructionists, a few of which are highlighted here, just to give a flavour of what is contemplated.

Says Heimbach:

Feminist author, Shulamith Firestone, claims, "the family is ... directly connected to – is even the cause of – the ills of the larger society." Feminist social critic Kate Millet has said, "The complete destruction of traditional marriage and the nuclear family is the *revolutionary or utopian* goal of feminism." And feminist scholar and University of Southern California professor, Judith Stacey, believes, "Perhaps the postmodern *family of women* will take the lead in burying The Family at long last. The Family is a concept derived from faulty theoretical premises and an imperialistic logic, which even at its height never served the best interests of women, their children, or even many men."[27]

Heimbach also quotes

Michael Swift, who styles himself a "gay revolutionary", zealously declar[ing], "The family unit – spawning ground of lies, betrayals, mediocrity, hypocrisy and violence – will be abolished. The family unit, which only dampens imagination and curbs free will, must be eliminated. Perfect boys will be conceived and grown in the genetic laboratory. They will be bonded together in communal setting, under the control and instruction of homosexual savants." And Franklin Kameny, founder of the gay movement in Washington, D.C., considers the very idea of *family* to be dangerously pernicious. Says Kameny, "the notion of the family … is enmeshed in a web … of religious, moral and theological precepts, all of which serve needlessly, harmfully, and perniciously to bind, limit, and restrain individuals in the exercise of their freedoms to enter into choices as to their intimate relationships."[28]

All of this alerts us to the fact that if same-sex marriage is legalised, the attack on traditional marriage and the family will be ongoing and relentless. And children, who have a profound right to both a mum and a dad, as we have stressed, will be among the ultimate casualties. So will be the moral fibre of our whole culture and civilisation.

Religious freedom imperilled

Beyond all that, religious freedom and conviction will be wrongfully constrained to give way to constitutional law. In reality what will happen, as is already happening for example in Canada, is that, with church and religious groupings outside the new constitutional norm, the stage gets set for endless legal disputes, collisions, and conflicts between church/religions and the state. To deny, actively oppose or refuse to cooperate with the new norm, on grounds of conscience or conviction, will be to deny people their new constitutional rights and be in breach of the law. For Christian pastors to preach against homosexual behaviour or same-sex marriage, if that is their understanding of the Bible's teaching, can be taken as hate-speech punishable by law. And that most certainly is a breach of religious freedom.

Likewise, courts can punish dissenting non-conformist schoolteachers who refuse to teach gay sex or gay marriage as required in school curricula. So too parents refusing to let their kindergarten children be introduced at school to explicit gay teaching about sexuality will be legally punishable and held to be intolerant, discriminators, or homophobic. Thus can unprecedented "sexual dogma" for children become acceptable, or even mandatory, in a nation's schools, while so-called "religious dogma" or instruction be ruled out. This is perilous social engineering as unacceptable as anything our apartheid years produced here in South Africa.

Incidentally, on all these grounds above, court cases are currently underway in Canada and Scandinavia. South Africa would surely follow suit. Church and state will be set for endless conflict, collision and even a new era of civil disobedience. And if people of religious conviction protest enough, then religion could finally become the enemy to be taken down or suppressed in some way or driven from the public square.

Time to say no

That's why, for all these reasons, the time is now for the church everywhere, for civil society and for both the state and its courts, to say "No" to same-sex marriage and preserve that which, in spite of failures and weaknesses, has stood the test of multiple millennia from creation until now.

The fact is that ultimately what lies beyond gay marriage is no marriage at all.

End Notes

1. For this vivid image of marriage as "civic glue" and for other insights incorporated into this chapter, I am much indebted to Advocate Iain Benson, director of the Institute for Cultural Renewal in Canada, and now residing in France.

2. Alan Sears and Craig Osten, *The Homosexual Agenda: Exposing the principal threat to religious freedom today* (Nashville: Broadman and Holman, 2003), 94, quoted in Erwin W. Lutzer, *The Truth about Same-Sex Marriage* (Chicago: Moody Publishers, 2004), 29.

3. Sears and Osten, 90, quoted in Lutzer, 28.

4. Advocate Iain Benson played a significant role in this case, where the nature and definition of the secular was in purview and where the ruling prevailed that the secular was inclusive of religion, rather than exclusive.

5. Stanley Kurtz, "The End of Marriage in Scandinavia", *The Weekly Standard*, February 2, 2004, <http://www.weeklystandard.com/Content/Public/Articles/000/000/003/660zypwj.asp>, March 5, 2006.

6. Kurtz, "The End of Marriage in Scandinavia."

7. Kurtz, "The End of Marriage in Scandinavia."

8. Kurtz, "The End of Marriage in Scandinavia."

9. Stanley Kurtz, "Standing Out", *National Review Online*, February 23, 2006, <http://www.nationalreview.com/kurtz/kurtz200602230800.asp>, March 5, 2006.

10. Kurtz, "Standing Out."

11. Kurtz, "The End of Marriage in Scandinavia."

12. G. K. Chesterton, *The Superstition of Divorce*, originally published in 1920, now available online from, for example: <http://www.hismercy.ca/content/ebooks/The.Superstition.of.Divorce-G.K.Chesterton.pdf>, March 5, 2006.

13. Margaret Somerville, "What About the Children?", *Divorcing Marriage: Unveiling the dangers in Canada's new social experiment*, Daniel Cere and Douglas Farrow, eds. (Montreal and Kingston: McGill-Queen's University Press, 2004), 78.

14. Kurtz, "The End of Marriage in Scandinavia."

15. Daniel R. Heimbach, "Deconstructing the Family to Justify Lust" (unpublished paper), 22.

16. Joseph Daniel Unwin, *Hopousia: Or the sexual and economic foundations of a new society* (London: George Allen and Unwin, 1940), 82-83, quoted in Heimbach, 24.

17. Joseph Daniel Unwin, *Sex and Culture* (London: Oxford University Press, 1934), 382, quoted in Heimbach, 24.

18. Pitirim Sorokin, *The American Sex Revolution* (Boston: Peter Sargent Publishers, 1956), 77-105, quoted in Timothy J. Dailey, PhD, "The Slippery Slope of Same-Sex 'Marriage'", Family Research Council, March 2, 2006, <http://www.frc.org/get.cfm?i=BC04C02>, March 6, 2006.

19. Stanley Kurtz, "Dissolving Marriage", *National Review Online*, February 3, 2006, <http://www.nationalreview.com/kurtz/kurtz200602030805.asp>, March 6, 2006.

20. Stanley Kurtz, "Here Come the Brides", *The Weekly Standard*, December 26, 2005, <http://www.weeklystandard.com/Content/Public/Articles/000/000/006/494pqobc.asp>, March 5, 2006.

21. "Polygamy" technically refers to either a husband with multiple wives, or a wife with multiple husbands. To be more precise, "polygyny" is a husband with multiple wives and "polyandry" is a wife with multiple husbands. But, since these latter two terms are not frequently used, we will employ the more widely understood word polygamy.

22. John-Henry Westen, "Gay Activists Ask Canada to Lower Age of Consent for Anal Sex, National Post Agrees", LifeSite, February 14, 2006, <http://www.lifesite.net/ldn/2006/feb/06021403.html>, March 6, 2006.

23. Heimbach, 6.

24. Stanley Kurtz, "Beyond Gay Marriage", *The Weekly Standard*, August 4, 2003, <http://www.weeklystandard.com/Content/Public/Articles/000/000/002/938xpsxy.asp?pg=2>, March 5, 2006.

25. Kurtz, "Beyond Gay Marriage."

26. Pierre de Vos, "Same-Sex Sexual Desire and the Re-Imagining of the South African Family", *South African Journal of Human Rights*, Vol. 20, Part 2 (2004).

27. Heimbach, 3.

28. Heimbach, 4.

Chapter Seven

ABORTION – A MAJOR ETHICAL DILEMMA IN OUR TIME

We come now to the vexed and emotive topic of abortion. And indeed it is an issue few can avoid, with between 50 million and 60 million abortions (legal and illegal) taking place in the world each year. On average, 130,000 infants are aborted every day. This is 6,278 every hour or 105 every minute. This is not far off two per second! And these are only the reported cases. Then there is the existence – even if rare – in the United States of partial-birth abortions, when the baby is destroyed in the birth canal a few minutes before it would have been born. This horrific practice is surely infanticide, hardly different than if the doctor waited a couple of minutes until the baby was in his hands.

Importance of presuppositions

In facing the abortion dilemma and seeking a direction for the answer, we must start, I believe, in the presuppositional worlds of those seeking answers. If we live in a godless, random universe which is simply the accidental result of impersonal energy, plus time, plus chance, then logically there are no ethical, moral or religious factors anywhere which need be taken into account, because there is no absolute moral or spiritual or transcendent reference point to which we have accountability or from which we derive our origins.

But if one's presuppositional world includes a creator, whose creatures we are, a God, in whose image we are made, and to whom we are finally accountable, plus authoritative Scriptures whose principles are morally and ethically determinative for the believer, plus a Christ who is Lord of all, then the abortion issue will have a different kind of answer determined by these supernaturalist, as against naturalist, presuppositions.

Commenting on how our modern world is putting to death millions of offspring, Everett Koop, former surgeon general of the United States and theologian Francis Schaeffer wrote:

Our society has justified taking their lives, even claiming it a virtue to do so. It has been said this is a new step in our progress toward a liberated humanity.

Such a situation has not come out of a vacuum. Each of us has an overall way of looking at the world, which influences what we do day by day. This is what we call a "world-view". And all of us have a world-view, whether we realise it or not. We act in accordance with our world-view, and our world-view rests on what to us is the ultimate truth.

What has produced the inhumanity we have been considering is that society in the West has adopted a world-view which says that all reality is made up only of matter. This view is sometimes referred to as philosophic materialism, because it holds that only *matter* exists; sometimes it is called naturalism, because it says that no supernatural exists. Humanism which begins from man alone and makes man the measure of all things usually is materialistic in its philosophy. Whatever the label, this is the underlying world-view of our society today. In this view the universe did not get here because it was created by a "supernatural" God. Rather, the universe has existed forever in some form, and its present form just happened as a result of chance events way back in time.[1]

But the problem here is that a material accidental universe can give us no basis for values, moral decisions or ethical principles. No real answers to the Big Questions about life, meaning, human destiny or the giving or taking of life can come from presuppositions which are philosophically materialistic.

We are simply left guessing. Morally at sea. Ethically adrift.

The alternative, the vastly better alternative I believe, is to try to think Christianly and from the presupposition of a world made and owned by God. In fact what is involved here for the Christian is our whole worldview, our understandings of God, the human species, creation, divine sovereignty, and the value and sanctity of human life. At issue too is whether God is really the one with final right and authority to give life or end it.

To terminate human life is a massive and vastly presumptuous step to take. No wonder Mother Theresa could thunder in these terms:

...only God can decide life and death... That is why abortion is such a terrible sin. You are not only killing life, but putting self before God;

> yet people decide who has to live and who has to die. They want to make themselves almighty God. They want to take the power of God in their hands. They want to say, "I can do without God. I can decide." That is the most devilish thing that a human hand can do...[2]

That's a pretty strong word – devilish. She likewise spoke forcefully on abortion at a National Prayer Breakfast some years ago in Washington, D.C., in the presence and to the discomfort of President Bill and Mrs Hillary Clinton: "Not abortion, but adoption: Give me your unwanted babies and I will find homes where they can be adopted."

The fact is that, however one views the human embryo, all have to agree that it is living and that the life which is there is human life. So our view of human life is involved when we seek to assess the relationship between unborn and new born children.

Everett Koop and Francis Schaeffer, in *Whatever Happened to the Human Race?* write: "Of all the subjects relating to the erosion of the sanctity of life, abortion is the keystone."[3] And they call it "an evil as great as any practised in human history."[4]

A complex and sensitive subject

That said, one must readily acknowledge at the outset that the abortion issue is highly sensitive and exceedingly complex, especially in the context of a promiscuous society where biblical norms for marriage and sexuality are increasingly violated or set aside, hence the reality of large numbers of unplanned and unwanted pregnancies. This sets the stage for endless tough choices which, in the best of all possible worlds, people should not have to be making at all.

It is obviously not my place or intention to stand in judgement on women who, for whatever reasons, are personally confronted with the abortion dilemma. My heart reaches out to those who are traumatised because of unwanted pregnancies. Such situations of anguish, as I know from counselling, require our deepest compassion and care. In fact, my wife, Carol, and I faced it very personally in 1976 when severe complications arose in Carol's pregnancy with our son, Martin, and certain doctors advised abortion. With Carol's own life at risk at one point, not to mention the infant's, we faced the matter very existentially.

When I see my strapping young 30-year-old son now, I rejoice with joy unspeakable that we made the choices we did under God and refused abortion. But the agonies can be awesome, as we can well testify. And so to the question, "to abort or not to abort"?

Rights and wrongs of rights

One of our initial concerns relates to how and where the notion of human rights comes into this debate. It is well known that those arguing in favour of the right to abortion emphasise the human rights of the mother and her right to choose in matters relating to herself and her own body. "Not the Church, not the State, let the woman decide her fate!"[5] says the cry. Those opposing abortion stress the rights of the unborn and especially his or her right to life. One side stresses the mother's right to avoid personal, social or financial trauma if the pregnancy proceeds. The other side stresses the rights of the defenceless unborn child to come into the world and move into the enjoyment of his or her humanness.

One way out is to distance ourselves totally from rights. This view asserts that the language of rights only complicates the issue, because one set of rights is simply set in opposition to another, with each set neutralising the other.

The more vital consideration is to ask where our so-called human rights come from in the first place. The Christian affirms that our human rights are conferred on us as part of the creation ordinance of God. No state or government confers these – whether on mother or child or John Citizen. Otherwise that same state or government which gave these rights can remove them. The Christian says, "No, these rights cannot be removed because they come from our Maker and are inherent in our creation by God."

This is to say that if a woman who finds herself with an unwanted pregnancy, for whatever reason, and pleads her rights, she should only do so with reference to her Creator as the originator of those rights and as the One who also gives rights to the unborn. She cannot decide purely individually or autonomously as if either she herself or the infant within her is not part of the divine creation. "You are not your own", says the apostle Paul; "you were bought with a price. So glorify God in your body" (1 Corinthians 6:19-20).

The key issue

This brings us to the key issue which depends on the one essential question: *When does the foetus become a person in his or her own right?* This question is different from asking when the life of the human being begins, which is a strictly biological question. Clearly this life begins at conception, when the new being receives the genetic code. But the essential question, whether or not the foetus is a person, is not biological. It is theological. If the foetus is, in fact, to be considered a person from conception, it must follow that abortion in normal circumstances is not morally acceptable. If, on the other hand, a foetus is considered to be a person only at some later date, then the question becomes, "When? At what stage? How do we know? And by what authority?"

Of course we recognise that different people have defined personhood in many different ways. For some (e.g., the late Carl Sagan, an astronomer) it is seen in the *ability to think*. Brain waves with regular patterns typical of adult human brains appear in the foetus about the thirtieth week of pregnancy. Others, such as the U.S. Supreme Court in its historic *Roe vs. Wade* ruling in 1973, have chosen *"viability"*, or the point when the baby can live independently of the woman, as the defining characteristic of personhood, a moment which, of course, with all our scientific advances, is moving earlier and earlier in the pregnancy process. Koop and Schaeffer point out in their objections to the viability principle that these relate not only to morals but to logic:

> It is impossible for anyone to say when a developing fetus becomes viable, that is, has the ability to exist on its own. Smaller and smaller premature infants are being saved each year! There was a day when a 1000-gram preemie had no chance; now 50 percent of preemies under 1000 grams are being saved. Theoretically, there once was a point beyond which technology could not be expected to go in salvaging premature infants – but with further technological advances, who knows what the limits may be! The eventual possibilities are staggering.

The logical approach is to go back to the sperm and the egg. A sperm has twenty-three chromosomes; even though it is alive and can fertilize an egg, it can never make another sperm. An egg also has twenty-three chromosomes, and it can never make another egg. Thus, we have sperm that cannot reproduce and eggs that cannot reproduce unless they get together. Once the union of a sperm and an egg occurs and the twenty-three chromosomes of each are brought together into one cell that has forty-six chromosomes, that one cell has all the DNA (the whole genetic code) that will, if not interrupted, make a human being.

Our question to a proabortion doctor who would not kill a *newborn* baby is this: "Would you then kill this infant a minute before he was born, or a minute before that, or a minute before that, or a minute before that? At what point in time can one consider life to be worthless and the next minute precious and worth saving?"[6]

Other people reject the viability route and put forward the idea that a foetus should not be considered a person until such time as it takes on sufficient characteristics so as to be *"visibly recognisable as a human foetus"*.

All these definitions of personhood are debatable at different points in different ways, but they also all share one common fault, namely the very questionable assumption, as already mentioned, that personhood is not in the very essence and nature of the human cell. While not all Christians agree, many would feel that the biblical view sees personhood as a lasting identity going on even into eternity and given to us by God from conception when sperm joins with ovum to form one living cell, smaller than a grain of salt. This new cell of life already contains the complex genetic blueprint for every detail of human development, including the child's sex, hair and eye colour, height, skin tone, etc. It is also worth noting here that even at the twelfth week (when, by South African law, the decision is still entirely up to the woman), the foetus can swallow, wrinkle its forehead, curl its toes, exercise its muscles, turn its head, close its mouth, clench its fists and ingest amniotic fluid to develop its respiratory system. By thirteen weeks, the miniature baby and the complete embryo is in place.

And even if personhood for the fertilised embryo is contested by contrary voices and it is argued that we cannot attribute to the embryo the qualities of the end product, nor see the rights of the end product as already belonging to the beginning, nevertheless we can say for sure that if we do indeed treat the unborn as persons, we will later know them as people! In other words, the unborn, by paradox, is in process of becoming what he or she already is, namely a person. In any event what is here is human life, not animal life, and therefore uniquely loved by God. At conception, as the old language says, "the woman is with child", not "with blob". To that notion, I believe, we must hold.

This is a posture which has been held by both ancient Judaism and the Christian Church from the beginning until more recent times when on this, as on other things, there has been a crisis of nerve.

Creation and personhood in the Scriptures

In the Genesis text, the highest point in creation was reached as God made both men and women in His own image (Genesis 1:26-27). Only human life has been created by God to possess His image and to be able to walk, talk, and share both earthly life and eternity with the creator. Moreover, from the moment of fertilisation, the indisputable fact remains that here is *human* life, rather than animal life. The embryo or foetus that is aborted is a *human* embryo or foetus and the blood shed is *human* blood. Here, moreover, is the life of an emerging person and, in abortion, one is extinguishing the life of such a being.

So we can't say that the foetus is a non-human mass of tissue. After all, he or she has a head and a body, a beating heart, separate nervous and circulation systems, his or her own skeleton, plus musculature, brain, heart and other vital organs. All this makes it very difficult for a woman to say that the foetus is part of her body and therefore dispensable by her if she so wishes, as she might do with her tonsils or appendix.

Personhood in the Scriptures

The idea that personhood is a lasting identity starting at conception is, I believe, supported throughout both the New and the Old Testaments. Says Isaiah, "The Lord called me from the womb" (49:1). Paul, for his part, can write of Him "who set me apart before I was born and called me through his grace" (Galatians1:15). Jeremiah 1:5 reads: "Before I formed you in the womb I knew you, and before you were born I consecrated you; I appointed you a prophet to the nations." In Luke 1:15, the Angel Gabriel says of John the Baptist that "he shall be filled with the Holy Spirit, even from his mother's womb." The story of Mary and Elizabeth's meeting in Luke 1:39-45 is also instructive where we read that John the Baptist leapt in Elizabeth's womb when he heard Mary's greeting. Jesus himself was conceived by the Holy Spirit, which fixes God the Father's involvement with Jesus the Son from the time He was a single cell inside Mary's uterus (Matthew 1:18). These Scriptures and others establish the Bible's view that personhood most certainly extends into the pre-natal stage and, in some sense at least, to conception.

David is certain that the Lord has been his God even from his mother's womb: "Yet you brought me out of the womb ... from my mother's womb you have been my God" (Psalm 22:9,10 – NIV).

Psalm 139 is one of the most dramatic passages of all, where David says: "For you created my inmost being; you knit me together in my mother's womb. I praise you because I am fearfully and wonderfully made; your works are wonderful, I know that full well. My frame was not hidden from you when I was made in the secret place. When I was woven together in the depths of the earth, your eyes saw my unformed body" (Psalm 139:13-16 – NIV).

John Stott, in his book, *Issues Facing Christians Today*, asserts that Psalm 139 contains three essential truths relevant to the abortion issue. First is the idea that a person is a *creation* of God. "You created my inmost being, you knit me together in my mother's womb", says verse 13. Stott's second point is *continuity*, as he notes that the psalmist refers to the past, present, future, and pre-natal stage, and "in all four stages ... he refers to himself as 'I'. He who is thinking and writing as a grown man has the same personal identity as the foetus in the womb. He is aware of no discontinuity between his antenatal and postnatal being."[7]

Stott points to *communion* as the third truth expressed in Psalm 139: "It is the same God who created him, who now sustains him, knows him and loves him, and who will forever hold him fast."[8] Stott further notes that, *"What makes us a person is not that we know God, but that he knows us; not that we love God but that He set His love on us. So each of us was already a person in our mother's womb, because already then God knew us and loved us."*[9]

Is abortion ever acceptable?

This is the crunch question. Inevitably opinions vary, even among Christians. And all Christian believers will have to try to reach their own chosen posture in integrity before the Lord, before the teachings of Scripture, and before the tough and often traumatic realities of the real world around us. The range of options are as follows:

So-called pro-choice

This says that it is the woman's choice as believer or unbeliever what she will do with her own pregnancy. For such a one, the points made above in this essay are, I believe, worthy of serious consideration. For me, that choice must be made with God as Creator in purview. For the unmarried, of course, the biblical choice also requires her not to have sex outside of marriage in the first place.

The absolutist position

No abortion under any circumstances – not even following incest or rape – is accepted unless the mother's own life is threatened. For many, such as James Dobson of Focus on the Family, this would be the logical consequence of the line presented in this essay. It is a posture much to be respected but requiring great spiritual fortitude.

The legal line

This follows whatever the law of any given country allows.

Anti-abortion but moderated by compassionate flexibility

This position basically sees abortion as an infraction of the Sixth Commandment – "Thou shalt not kill" – but acknowledges that, in reality, living as we do in a fallen and sin-infected world, the taking of life – as in self-defence or sometimes capital punishment – may be countenanced. In the case of abortion, while normally morally wrong, it may in certain cases call for compassionate flexibility rather than intractable rigidity as the lesser of two evils, as when pregnancy constitutes a serious threat to a woman's life or her physical or mental health; or in cases of rape or incest; or as a consequence of alleged unlawful carnal intercourse with a woman having a permanent mental handicap or defect. These are issues which must be struggled with and agonised over in each individual case and answers sought before God, His people and one's family.

South African theologian Klaus Nürnberger, commenting on the "lesser of two evils" predicament, notes that: "An emergency measure may not become the norm. Choice of the lesser evil is only justified as long as, and to the extent that, one can do nothing about preventing the greater evil. Choice of the lesser evil presupposes a commitment to overcome the greater evil, thus making the lesser evil redundant. If we built up the immune system of the society, we would not have to administer bitter pills."[10]

Adoption, not abortion

This, as we've said, was always Mother Teresa's great cry. It is not really a totally separate option but it would seek, amid all the other options, to plead with mothers – especially unmarried ones – who have an unwanted pregnancy to go to a pregnancy crisis centre or an adoption agency and explore the adoption option. So many childless parents want to adopt a child. Surely to grant them that desire and save the unborn from abortion is a far better path to take. Hence Mother Teresa's great and oft-repeated cry already mentioned: "Adoption not abortion. Send me your unwanted children. I will find homes for them."

Conclusion

My personal conclusion blends the last two options above, and affirms that abortion is not God's way and, except under the most severe constraints of, for example, rape or incest or threat to the mother's life, it should not be countenanced.

But the necessity of caring compassionately and with deep understanding for women facing unwanted pregnancies rests heavily on all, especially Christian believers and the Church as a whole. This care must also be extended in love even to those who cannot subscribe to the kind of line taken in this chapter.

Nonetheless, we feel constrained to affirm that abortion is not the right answer to the problem of an unwanted pregnancy. Adoption is by far the better route. Rather than proliferate abortion clinics, vastly preferable would be a new government- and church-financed multiplication of pregnancy crisis centres and adoption agencies offering wise, sensitive and godly counselling along this line. I believe this is important not only for the sake of the baby, but for the pregnant woman as well, as the latest research out of New Zealand has demonstrated unequivocally that "young women who have abortions subsequently experience elevated rates of suicidal behaviors, depression, substance abuse, anxiety, and other mental problems."[11] Professor David Fergusson, a psychologist and director of the Christchurch Health and Development Study of 500 women over their lives from birth to 25 years – which controlled for any other contributing factors – said: "Abortion is a traumatic life event; that is, it involves loss, it involves grief, it involves difficulties. And the trauma may, in fact, predispose people to having mental illness."[12] Lest anyone suspect Prof Fergusson of being connected with pro-life or Christian entities, he said after the release of the study: "I remain pro-choice. I am not religious. I am an atheist and a rationalist. The findings did surprise me, but the results appear to be very robust because they persist across a series of disorders and a series of ages."[13]

I include the results of this study not to add further trauma to anyone faced with an unwanted pregnancy, but only to emphasise that what might seem like a helpful solution in the form of ending the pregnancy, could well lead to more mental and emotional anguish than could delivering the child and either releasing him or her through adoption, or seeking to keep the child and raise him or her even in difficult circumstances.

Another word of counsel to young women contemplating abortion: May I cry to you before you take that route, to go to a doctor and get an ultrasound scan of the infant in your womb. As you see that little life, a real human, though miniature, and all in place with a beating heart and all, the chances are strong you will reconsider abortion and decide either to keep the infant or go the adoption route.

Above all, we register afresh that adoption protects the inestimable worth which attaches under God to the defenceless unborn. And this inestimable worth of the unborn is what makes abortion so highly questionable in almost all circumstances.

End Notes

1. C. Everett Koop and Francis Schaeffer, *Whatever Happened to the Human Race?* (Westchester, Illinois: Crossway Books, 1979), 13, 78-79.
2. Desmond Doig, *Mother Teresa: Her people and her work* (London: Collins, 1976), 162, quoted in John Stott, *Issues Facing Christians Today* (London: Marshall Pickering, 1990), 308.
3. Koop and Schaeffer, 13.
4. Koop and Schaeffer, 78.
5. John Stott, *Issues Facing Christians Today* (London: Marshall Pickering, 1990), 313.
6. Koop and Schaeffer, 16-17.
7. Stott, 316.
8. Stott, 316.
9. Stott, 316, italics mine.
10. Klaus Nürnburger, "When is killing justified? A comparison between abortion, war and capital punishment" (unpublished paper), October 1, 1996.
11. "Abortion Causes Mental Disorders: New Zealand Study May Require Doctors to Do Fewer Abortions", Elliot Institute for Social Sciences Research/AfterAbortion.org, February 9, 2006, <http://www.afterabortion.info/news/Fergusson.htm>, March 5, 2006
12. Nick Grimm, reporter, "Higher rise of mental health problems after abortion: report", *The 7:30 Report*, Australian Broadcasting Corporation TV program transcript, Broadcast: January 3, 2006, <http://www.abc.net.au/7.30/content/2006/s1541543.htm>, February 14, 2006.
13. Grimm, "Higher rise of mental health problems after abortion: report."

Chapter Eight

EUTHANASIA – IS THERE A PLACE FOR MERCY KILLING?

We come now to explore the evocative and emotive topic of euthanasia. Some call it mercy-killing or physician-assisted suicide. Everett Koop and Francis Schaeffer comment: "Here we come to the next logical step that follows from abandoning the biblical perspective that mankind is unique, in that all men, women, and children are made in the image of God. The wide-open door of abortion-on-demand leads naturally to infanticide which leads naturally to euthanasia."[1]

In other words, if one can take life at one end of the spectrum (the unborn infant), why not at the other end (the aged person)? With "life as a continuum from conception until natural death", they ask: "Since life is being destroyed before birth, why not tamper with it on the other end?"

> Will a society which has assumed the right to kill infants in the womb – because they are unwanted, imperfect, or merely inconvenient – have difficulty in assuming the right to kill other human beings, especially older adults who are judged unwanted, deemed imperfect physically or mentally, or considered a possible social nuisance?
>
> The next candidates for arbitrary reclassification as nonpersons are the elderly. This will become increasingly so as the proportion of the old and weak in relation to the young and strong becomes abnormally large, due to the growing antifamily sentiment, the abortion rate, and medicine's contribution to the lengthening of the normal life span.[2]

Initially euthanasia would seem to be a subject relevant only to those near the end of life or to the loved ones of people in such a predicament. But it cannot be separated from the wider issues of the purposes and ends of life, plus the whole issue of God – His sovereignty over life and death and His relationship with humans.

Some countries have already legalised euthanasia: the Netherlands, Belgium and Colombia. Other places, such as the Northern Territories of Australia and the U.S. state of Oregon have enacted laws allowing certain forms of assisted suicide, though some of these are still in legal contention. Perhaps the key problem relates to the basis in all of these countries for their decisions, because in Western countries there is no current consensus about the basis for ethical decisions. This brings us by way of prelude to the central problem.

The cultural crux of the problem

The loss of a Judaeo-Christian ethical base to our society affects all ethical issues, including homosexuality, abortion and obviously this one under purview now. The problem is that we are living in a unique cultural moment in the Western world. Underneath other major cultures there are religious assumptions, whether emanating from Hinduism, Islam, etc., even as there were from Christianity in the past in our Western culture. But now in our neo-pagan, postmodern Western culture, those assumptions are going or gone. This shattering reality means that less and less is there any core set of values with wide assent which can be invoked to regulate our culture's competing voices, interests and practices as they jostle one another for supremacy. In consequence we are ethically adrift. This aggravates our problem.

What is euthanasia?

The Oxford Dictionary describes euthanasia as "the act of causing somebody to die gently and without pain, especially when they are suffering from a painful, incurable disease." Euthanasia proper does not in essence include the removal of a person from a life support system, although some call this *passive euthanasia* in contrast to *active euthanasia*. Perhaps it is less confusing to confine the term primarily to acts which hasten the death of someone who would otherwise still live. Even so, we note that much secular ethical discussion focuses on whether there is a morally significant distinction between causing death (active euthanasia) and allowing death to happen (passive euthanasia).

Commenting on this in a letter to the author, Dr Albu van Eeden of Doctors for Life in South Africa, helpfully compared active and passive euthanasia saying:

There are two forms of active euthanasia: The traditional form where the doctor gives the patient an injection or something similar to kill the patient. The second form is called "doctor-assisted suicide" – where the doctor gives the patient medicine with which to commit suicide.

Firstly there is a difference in the agent. In passive euthanasia the agent is the disease. The doctor stands back and allows the disease to take its course. In active euthanasia the agent is the doctor. He kills the patient by giving him/her an injection etc. Usually it is accepted that extraordinary treatment can be terminated (under certain conditions) and it would not be considered active euthanasia, e.g., switching off a ventilator in a brain dead patient. In such a case the disease will kill the patient. Stopping ordinary treatment like food and water would be considered active euthanasia. One would not be keeping someone "artificially" alive by giving him/her food and nutrition. Actually food and water is not even treatment, as everybody needs food and water in order to live.

The intent in passive euthanasia is to stop prolonging the dying process – the doctor's goal is not in the first place the death of the patient. If the doctor switched the machine off and the patient remained alive, the doctor would only be too happy. In active euthanasia his intent is the death of the patient.

The attitude in passive euthanasia is an attitude of humility and recognition. The doctor accepts that he is not God and unable to keep the patient indefinitely alive. In active euthanasia the attitude is one of taking control.

In passive euthanasia the means is allowing the patient to die. In active euthanasia the means is killing.

Doctors for Life can support a patient's right to refuse treatment, but that is far removed from the right to request help to die.[3]

What does alive mean?

What does "alive" mean when modern medical knowledge can keep a body alive when the brain is dead? In the view of missionary doctor Gerrit ter Haar: "One cannot speak of life any more in such cases. Physiological brain death is irreversible and a person with a flat EEG (electroencephalogram) is no longer alive. The key factor here is that if it is scientifically and medically established that 'brain death' is irreversible and that breathing and heartbeat can only be maintained artificially, then lifting life support systems on 'the living dead' should not be considered as euthanasia proper."[4]

We know, of course, that the doctor is the servant of life, and the trust of both patient and relatives rests on this assurance. The patient knows the doctor is on his or her side. But is there a point with a person who is not brain dead when the doctor's "life" obligation ceases, as in an intolerably painful illness with no cure in sight? And what if the patient asks to be released from a living death? Some introduce the distinction between the prolongation of life and the prolongation of the act of dying. This is indeed a minefield.

Christian and humanist worldviews

We must, as we did when facing the abortion dilemma, start with the presuppositional worldviews of those seeking answers. Here we have two: the secular humanist-materialist (where matter in an accidental godless universe is the final reality) and the biblical (where final reality is the infinite-personal creator God who has revealed himself to humanity in Jesus Christ and the Bible). These two worldviews, with their different "final reality" perceptions, stand in antithesis to each other. And being totally different concepts, they will bring forth two morally different conclusions both for society and for the individual. Starting with the human being and with no knowledge except what fallible human reason can conclude, the secular humanist can have no standards outside of himself.

"Utility above life" can then come in as a key principle to help decide life or death by euthanasia according to perceived usefulness. Such an unconscionable view is not illogical for ideological humanism where the human species is the measure of all things. This kind of contemporary humanism also goes well beyond the old justification for euthanasia of giving a good and quick death to the incredibly ill and suffering. Here mercy killing was for the sake of the sufferer. Now it can be considered in utilitarian categories for the convenience of those who are alive and left behind.

So, unless the Church raises a contrary voice, the day will be progressively carried in our neo-pagan age by utilitarianism (is this death useful to us?), or sentiment (is this suffering too much?) or choice (do you want the option to die now or to suffer on?).

But the Christian, starting with God and his Word, operates under divine principle and moral law, the creature under the Creator. The questions then are theological. "How does God see this? What does he want? What biblical principles are there to guide us in this matter? How can I obey my Lord and his Word?"

Fears and compassion behind the euthanasia impulse

A person in a state of suffering from a disease or nearing the end of life would likely be experiencing fears of one sort or another, such as:

Fear of pain
All people feel death is a painful reality. But actually in this day and age, there is little reason for a dying person to experience excruciating pain. The palliative care system in most developed countries (the only countries in which euthanasia is an issue) has become so effective that there are few maladies from which much of the pain cannot be very significantly alleviated. Even so, we tend to fear any pain.

Fear of abandonment
If treasured relationships for oldies are not maintained or they feel abandoned, then many would sooner die than exist in isolated suffering.

Fear of being a burden
For some, the idea that they are now going to need expensive and inconvenient help after a lifetime of being a provider is an absolute nightmare. "I would rather die than land on my kids", say many.

Fear of the process of dying
David Watson, the great English evangelist, once said to me when he was dying of cancer, "Because of Jesus I do not fear death, but I do rather fear the process of dying." So some feel, "Please accelerate the process."

All these fears are very real and valid. On the other side of the situation is the genuine compassion and concern which doctors and loved ones feel for the person who is suffering.

Compassionate concern in the healer or doctor towards the sufferer

If alleviating pain, suffering, and sickness is the main negative duty of medical practice, then serving the patient's highest health interests is the positive rationale of all medical treatment, and the central obligation of care-givers to their patients. Beneficence is the technical term in medical ethics. It is the easiest of all principles to ground in Christian faith, as part of the universal Christian obligation to love the neighbour, and surely your dying neighbour.

Autonomy and rights

In a society preoccupied with individual rights and personal autonomy, it does not surprise us that the debate over physician-assisted suicide focuses on the right to die. The word in medical ethics is autonomy. Interestingly enough, the US Supreme Court ruled on 26 June 1997, that "there is no constitutional right to die". We might want to die or to be helped to die, but that does not create a right to die. Then-Chief Justice William Rhenquist said that allowing doctors to use lethal medication to end lives conflicts with "our nation's history, legal tradition, and practices". Medically, respect for autonomy is most primarily expressed in the requirement of free and informed consent for medical procedures affecting one's life, health and well-being. In most countries this is enshrined in law and professional ethics. However, amid all the pleading of rights, we reiterate that this is not problematic for the Christian, provided all remember that our human rights are not self-given or self-defined or determined by majority vote. They come from God, are inherent in our creation, and to be exercised under him and according to his word. And our wants are not automatically our rights.

It is perhaps at this point instructive to note some of the rights claimed in this matter:

Right to refuse treatment
The concern expressed in this cry is that people do not want to be forced to take pharmaceuticals or undergo massive, painful and disfiguring treatment against their will. This is Christianly acceptable. Beyond that, many ethicists feel that even with the irreversibly brain-dead, only the family, not the doctor, should have the final right to decide whether support systems be removed or not.

Right to die with dignity
The desire for this is deep, God-given and to be honoured.

Right to control
A lot of the euthanasia debate is about control. We want as much as possible to control our own destinies, even to the point of controlling when and how we die. However, most Christians would contend that sanctioning active euthanasia would have the reverse effect. Instead of allowing individuals to make choices, it would rob the right of choice from those most vulnerable. And once legalised, it can easily be manipulated by the powerful. More than that, suggestions to the weak or unwilling that their time on earth should come to an end could be so firmly asserted, that they would be pathetically acceded to. The perils are obvious and awesome. Beyond that, the Christian must assert that final and ultimate control is to be left in God's hands.

Sanctity of life
This is one of the foundational principles for those who oppose euthanasia, just as for those actively opposing abortion. Being created in God's image not only provides a person with dignity, but also affirms the notion that the sanctity of life has strong biblical affirmation.

For medical people, the sanctity of life principle makes motivation a critical factor in the euthanasia debate. Thus if a doctor with the sole motivation of alleviating pain allows doses of morphine or whatever, which he knows in accumulative terms will finally be fatal, he would not surely be violating the sanctity of life, because he is not trying to bring about death but alleviate pain. But if, "playing God", he or she administers the lethal dose with the clear motivation of killing the patient, that indeed violates the sanctity of life because the purpose is to terminate life. The distinction may be subtle but is critically important, the one motivation being morally receivable and the other morally perilous.

Key biblical principles to underline

Obviously euthanasia was not an issue that directly confronted those who lived in biblical times, so we have no scriptural references specifically addressing the issue. However, let us underline some relevant principles:

The sovereignty of God in Christ over life and death

This speaks of the final "in-chargeness" of God as the one who gives life and who takes it. "This is God's call", said a doctor to me when my mother was dying. Said the Lord to Hezekiah: "I will add 15 years to your life" (2 Kings 20:6). The time of his birth and death was God's decision. The Psalmist knew this when he affirmed: "My times are in your hand" (Psalm 31:15). In other words, "you, Lord, know when I will die". In the New Testament we also have Jesus saying, "I have the keys of life and death..." (Revelation 1:18). He also said, "The very hairs of your head are numbered" (Matthew 10:30). And Peter could even call him "The author of life" (Acts 3:15). In other words, both our life destiny and our death destiny are in his hands. To interfere with that is no light matter.

Divine plans and will

A corollary of the above is that God has plans for us and for all people which we should not thwart. Said the Lord through Jeremiah, "I know the plans I have for you" (Jeremiah 29:11). "You are not your own", says Paul (1 Corinthians 6:19). This means we cannot take our own lives or wilfully take the innocent life of another. (Self-defence or capital punishment are, of course, separate debates.)

The dealings of God with the dying

A senior nursing sister told me of the deep sense she had when her husband was dying that God was doing deep things with him and he was doing deep things with God. Spending hours and days in late 1997 and early 1998 at the bedside of my dying mother, I had the profound sense of eternal things happening with her right up to the last minutes – though both she and I were longing for weeks beforehand for her release. But God had His time and was dealing with her and she with Him to the very last. To interrupt that eternal business prematurely is not the province of humans. Says Paul, "Everyone who calls on the name of the Lord will be saved" (Romans 10:13). To terminate someone's life prematurely could be to prevent the possibility of that call. We cannot do it.

The role in the Christian life of suffering
No one says suffering is good. It is evil and part of our fallen estate. But it is not a biblical principle to avoid all suffering at all costs, because our faith is often deepened and matured by the trials and sufferings that come our way (see James 1:12, 1 Peter 1:6). Take the seemingly inexplicable sufferings of Job. We now know that these had meaning in God's plan. We could seek to end suffering with the sufferer by ending life, but doctors might make a breakthrough cure, or God might supernaturally heal him or her on their death-bed! I have known and met such cases.

The ministry of the dying
While we may major on what we think we could or should, under God, be doing for the dying person, we also need to register what the Lord may still have for the dying person, under God, to do for us! "His ways are not our ways", and it seems the Lord will often do extra-ordinary, supernatural, eternal things through the dying person in the lives of his or her friends and family or nursing staff. Again we dare not interrupt God doing His thing in His way for His purposes.

The Dutch experiment
We alluded earlier to the Dutch experiment, the Netherlands being the first country to legalise euthanasia and the most daring in its deadly experimentation. How have things fared there?

"Shockingly" is the answer. In an article entitled "Now They Want to Euthanize Children", Wesley Smith, an attorney for the

International Task Force on Euthanasia and Assisted Suicide, writes: "Dutch doctors have been surreptitiously engaging in eugenic euthanasia of disabled babies for years ... doctors were killing approximately 8 percent of all infants who died each year in the Netherlands. That amounts to approximately 80-90 per year. ...At least 10-15 of these killings involved infants who did not require life-sustaining treatment to stay alive. The study found that a shocking 45 percent of neo-natologists and 31 percent of pediatricians who responded to questionnaires had killed infants."[5]

Smith concludes: "It took the Dutch almost 30 years for their medical practices to fall to the point that Dutch doctors are able to engage in the kind of euthanasia activities that got some German doctors hanged after Nuremberg. For those who object to this assertion by claiming that German doctors killed disabled babies during World War II without consent of parents, so too do many Dutch doctors: Approximately 21 percent of the infant euthanasia deaths occurred *without* request or consent of parents. Moreover, since when did parents attain the moral right to have their children killed?"[6]

Even more chilling is a report on "The Groningen Protocol", a "proposal of doctors in the Netherlands for the establishment of an 'independent committee' charged with selecting babies and other severely handicapped or disabled people for euthanasia." Evidently, "A parent's role is limited under the protocol. While experts and critics familiar with the policy said a parent's wishes to let a child live or die naturally most likely would be considered, they note that the decision must be professional, so rests with the doctors."[7]

In regard to the elderly, "Many old people now fear Dutch hospitals. More than 10 percent of senior citizens who responded to a recent survey, which did not mention euthanasia, volunteered that they feared being killed by their doctors without their consent."[8] Indeed, one Dutch GP was found guilty of the murder of an 84-year-old patient in 2001 and was not penalised: "The Amsterdam court that tried him said that Dr Wilfred van Oijen had made an 'error of judgment' but had acted 'honourably and according to his conscience,' showing compassion, in what he considered the interests of his patient... The Royal Dutch Medical Association (KNMG) has defended his action as having 'complete integrity,' claiming a 'huge emotional gulf' between it and the offence of murder."[9]

However...! One can see nightmarishly where the practice of active euthanasia can lead.

Conclusion

In sum, neither Christian conscience nor the Bible can sanction active, deliberate euthanasia. Its irrevocability, its interference with God as Lord of life and death, its interruption of what the dying person may be doing in the Spirit for others, its terminating of the sufferer's eternal business with his or her maker and the sanctity of life principle, all make it unacceptable. Key to our discussion is the matter of motive. The motive to relieve and ease pain and suffering is morally praiseworthy and vital. Anything else is morally and biblically unacceptable.

End Notes

1. C. Everett Koop and Francis A. Schaeffer, *Whatever Happened to the Human Race?* (Westchester, Illinois: Crossway Books, 1979), 53.
2. Koop and Schaeffer, 54.
3. Personal letter to the Author from Dr Albu van Eeden, 29 March 2005.
4. Personal letter to the Author from Dr Gerritt ter Haar, 12 March 1998.
5. Wesley J. Smith, "Now They Want to Euthanize Children", *The Weekly Standard*, September 13, 2004, <http://www.weeklystandard.com/Content/Public/Articles/000/000/004/006jszlg.asp>, March 3, 2006.
6. Smith, "Now They Want to Euthanize Children."
7. Hugh Hewitt, "Death by Committee", *The Weekly Standard*, December 2, 2004, <http://www.weeklystandard.com/Content/Public/Articles/000/000/004/983ynlcv.asp>, March 3, 2006.
8. Richard Miniter, "The Dutch Way of Death", *The Wall Street Journal*, April 28, 2001, <http://opinionjournal.com/editorial/feature.html?id=95000390>, March 3, 2006.
9. Tony Sheldon, "Dutch GP found guilty of murder faces no penalty", *British Medical Journal*, March 3, 2001, <http://bmj.bmjjournals.com/cgi/content/full/322/7285/509/a>, March 3, 2006

Chapter Nine

CAPITAL PUNISHMENT
– IS THERE STILL A PLACE FOR IT?

I remember some years back sitting in a meeting of church leaders discussing the issue of abortion. One minister was punting very strongly the right to life of the unborn. A comment was then made by one opponent of this line saying that he was incredulous that anyone could oppose abortion and then support the death penalty. "If you support life, you must support life consistently. It's hopeless philosophical inconsistency if you don't." As the discussion was degenerating into one of those typical South African exchanges with more heat than light, I decided not to gird my loins and contribute to the heat. But, had I done so, I would have sought to make two points.

- Holding as I do the view of Scripture as our supreme authority for all matters of faith and morals, the issue for me is not philosophical, but exegetical – i.e., not what is philosophically consistent for a secularist but what does the Bible say? And I refuse to have this lampooned as an obscurantist fundamentalism. It's simply a matter of seeking to take the Bible seriously.

- There is a significant difference between a totally innocent unborn child and a massively guilty criminal who has murdered one, two, or twenty people, perhaps with horrendous barbarism and brutality, possibly with sexual assault thrown in, and maybe even devilish deliberations, brutal violence and cruelty on top of it all. Like whoever raped and then murdered in cold blood the student-aged son and daughter of friends of mine, their only two children.

However, such points can only be preliminary in what is a desperately complex debate, rendered substantially more complex by three factors: first, the massive abuse of the death penalty in the past (especially in the apartheid era here in South

Africa). Second, the current crime pandemic in South Africa and the almost total disregard of the law and its penalties. And third, the fact that there are instances, probably in most countries, of people being sent to the gallows who subsequently are proven to have been not guilty.

Here in South Africa, with our endless record of extremely violent crime, it is not surprising that many are calling for the reintroduction of the death penalty as vigorously as others resist it. How should we think? Which way should we go? I venture here some tentative reflections. Being in a minefield, we must proceed carefully.

Preliminary considerations

First of all, what are we to say of a country like my own where there are some 25,000 murders a year, a rate of some 68 per day (11 times higher than the world average)? Surely it is not surprising that, having abolished the death penalty, our country now faces a clamour for its reintroduction. Is such a clamour valid?

As Christians, it would be a grave mistake to evaluate the debate over capital punishment based on fear or reactionary anger. Although there are certainly some basic practical factors to be considered, such as the effect of capital punishment has on deterring crime, it is essential that our perspective be informed first and foremost by moral and ethical considerations based on God's authoritative revelation in His Word. Based on what we know of God, of His holiness and justice, as well as His mercy and compassion, and based at least for the Christian on what the Scriptures say, we must evaluate whether capital punishment is a right response to the crime of murder before we ask whether it is an effective response.

Obviously this is one of the most complex ethical issues of our day and there are intelligent and thoughtful Christians on both sides of this debate. For myself, I touch it with great reluctance, but feel one has little option, seeing the matter is out there, in quite a big way, before the church and the secular public. So, difficult though it may be, I don't believe it can be evaded or avoided.

That said, I think there are five key questions needing both an initial and an ongoing reflection:

1. What do the Scriptures, both Old and New Testaments, exegetically teach about the death penalty?

2. Is capital punishment a deterrent and should this be an important consideration?

3. Are there sins or crimes which are deserving of the death penalty?

4. Do we in this country, or does any country looking at this issue, have a legal and state system able to administer such a drastic penalty equitably?

5. As to South Africa specifically, could our precarious political context and history cope with the reintroduction of the death penalty?

I list these five questions together so that we realistically hold before us both the ancient text of Scripture and the immediate context of the real situation before us. We are to scan the double horizon of both Word and world, both ideal and real, both the "then" and the "now", both the universal and the local, both the biblical context and the current context. Clearly I can't (who could?) attempt to resolve this matter completely, but perhaps we can contribute to an ongoing and necessary discussion.

What do the Scriptures say?

Old Testament teaching

Beginning in Genesis 9, at God's covenant with Noah and his descendants, the Old Testament does in fact establish the principle that certain sins must be punished with death. Genesis 9:5-6 reads: "For your lifeblood I will surely require a reckoning; of every beast I will require it and of man; of every man's brother I will require the life of man. Whoever sheds the blood of man, by man shall his blood be shed; for God made man in his own image."

A crime against humanity and God

This passage suggests that the murder of a fellow human being is a crime, not only against the victim, but against the Creator. Since murder is a crime against both humanity and God, there are in fact both temporal and divine consequences for such sin. God himself will punish sin ("I will surely require a reckoning"), but humankind also has a responsibility to punish ("by man shall his blood be shed"). This passage provides a moral context for the discussion of capital punishment by clearly establishing the monumental value and sanctity of human life. Here in the Old Testament, the *imago Dei* (image of God), with which humans are uniquely endowed, was understood to signify human life as so sacred that its destruction in God's eyes deserved both divine judgement and human punishment.

Mosaic Law

Old Testament Scripture also makes it clear that capital punishment was to be practised (and was practised) under the Mosaic Law. The Mosaic Law in fact prescribed the death penalty for eighteen different offences, including murder (Exodus 21: 12-14; Numbers 35:16-21), kidnapping (Exodus 21:16), rape of a married woman (Deuteronomy 22:25-29), adultery (Leviticus 20:10), rebelling against parents (Deuteronomy 21:18-21), as well as other sexual sins and violent crimes. However, only for the crime of intentional murder was the death penalty *mandatory*, and Old Testament scholars suggest that the penalty for the other seventeen specified sins was, in fact, commutable at a judge's discretion, but revealed the seriousness of the sins nevertheless. But for malicious, intentional murder, Numbers 35:31 makes it clear that a substitute or lesser sentence was not acceptable: "Moreover you shall accept no ransom for the life of a murderer, who is guilty of death; but he shall be put to death." In other words, Old Testament law saw the punishment for first-degree murder as unique, and not open to any degree of interpretation or commutation.

Contemporary application

The question of contemporary application of these Scriptures must naturally arise at this point. An obvious comeback must surely be: "If we are going to base our support of capital punishment for murder on Old Testament teachings, then why not the same punishment for the other seventeen sins?" One possible answer is that Bible scholars do make legitimate distinctions between the legislation given to Israel as a theocratic state under Moses and the more universal revelation given to the human race through Noah. While the New Testament church is not bound by all of the specific provisions of the Mosaic Law (e.g., dietary restrictions, animal sacrifice, etc.), the Noahic Covenant, including God's promise never again to flood the whole earth, applies, in principle, to the entire human race. The requirement that blood be shed as a reckoning for murder is based on the unchanging nature of humanity, which bears the image of the Divine. The significance of this must be emphasised. To talk about humanity being made in the image of God automatically takes us into a central theme of Scripture. One only needs to look through the Old Testament and into the New to see how profoundly this theology of humanity being made in the image of God undergirds other significant theologies: Christ as human representing God to us is probably the most amazing one of all (John 1; 2 Corinthians 4:4; Colossians 1:15), as well as the fact that Jesus' vicarious work restores us to that *imago Dei* role (Colossians 3:9-10). Therefore, one can never understate the incredible violation that murder is. And so to discuss its punishment is to discuss something quite unique amongst issues of responses to sin.

Of course, if one also subscribes, as I do, to the notion of Progressive Revelation (i.e., that God revealed Himself progressively from Old to New Testaments), then we would recognise that the New Testament over-ruled, for example, the Old Testament death penalty for adultery. But did it over-rule the death penalty *per se* for murder?

New Testament teaching
Jesus Christ, the Word made flesh, came as the fulfilment and Expositor Supreme of the Old Testament Law. Naturally, therefore, it is sometimes argued that Jesus' teaching and His own example of compassion, mercy and forgiveness override or

nullify the penalty required by the Mosaic Law and the Noahic Covenant.

Possibly the most instructive New Testament text in any discussion of capital punishment is Romans 13:1-7. In his discussion of the God-given authority of earthly rulers, the Apostle Paul writes: "For there is no authority except from God, and those that exist have been instituted by God ... for he is God's servant for your good. But if you do wrong, be afraid, for he does not bear the sword in vain; he is the servant of God to execute his wrath on the wrongdoer." (Romans 13:1b, 4)

The word "sword" (Greek: *machaira*) is used earlier in Paul's letter to indicate death (Romans 8:35), and the sword was used as an instrument of execution. It follows, therefore, that Paul uses the term to represent capital punishment. In the context of the passage, in which Paul describes the Christian's duty to obey earthly authorities, it seems that capital punishment is an element of the state's responsibility as an agent of God himself. God has entrusted human institutions with a great responsibility to carry out His justice on earth, just as He entrusted to Noah and his descendants in Genesis 9.

Scots-born scholar and biblical exegete, John Murray, one-time professor of systematic theology at Princeton Theological Seminary and then Westminster Seminary, comments on why those who break the law will feel "terror" or "fear" (Romans 13:3) before the state:

> The reason is that the magistrate "bears not the sword in vain". The sword which the magistrate carries as the most significant part of his equipment is not merely the sign of his authority but of his right to wield it in the infliction of that which a sword does. It would not be necessary to suppose that the wielding of the sword contemplates the infliction of the death penalty exclusively. It can be wielded to instil the terror of that punishment which it can inflict. It can be wielded to execute punishment that falls short of death. But to exclude the right of the death penalty when the nature of the crime calls for such is totally contrary to that which the sword signifies and executes. We need appeal to no more than New Testament usage to establish this reference. The sword is so frequently associated with death as the instrument of execution (cf. Matt. 26:52; Luke 21:24; Acts 12:2; 16:27; Heb. 11:34, 37; Rev. 13:10) that to exclude its use for this purpose in

this instance would be so arbitrary as to bear upon its face prejudice contrary to the evidence. "In vain" means to no purpose.

"For he is a minister of God, an avenger for wrath to him that doeth evil." In the first clause the ruler is said to be the minister of God for good. Now the same office is accorded to him for avenging evil. The parallelism is noteworthy – the same dignity and investiture belong to the ruler's penal prerogative as to his function in promoting good. This penal function is said to consist in being "an avenger unto wrath" to the evil-doer. This is the first time that the term "wrath" is used in reference to the civil magistrate. In verse 2 we found that the "judgment" alludes to the judgment of God of which the retribution executed by the civil magistrate is the expression and from which this retribution derives its sanction.[1]

This is tough stuff, and perhaps hard to receive but, notes Murray, "We see how divergent from biblical teaching is the sentimentality that substitutes the interests of the offender for the satisfaction of justice as the basis of criminal retribution."[2]

The famous biblical exegetes, William Sanday and Arthur Headlam in the *International Critical Commentary* on Romans, write: "The sword is the symbol of the executive and criminal jurisdiction of a magistrate, and is therefore used of the power of punishing inherent in the government."[3] They add that the state "exists positively for the well-being of the community, negatively to check evil by the infliction of punishment, and both these functions are derived from God."[4]

Professor F.F. Bruce, formerly of Manchester University, comments from his perspective on the state's responsibility "to execute his [God's] wrath on the wrongdoer" (Romans 13:4). The state

…is charged with a function which has been explicitly forbidden to the Christian (xii. 17a, 19). …It is plain that Paul envisages two quite distinct spheres of "service" to God. "The sanction that the Bible, here and elsewhere, gives to the forcible restraint of evil puzzles many modern Christians, because of its apparent contradiction to Christ's way of love and His precept of non-resistance to evil. But this comes from failing to distinguish the preservation of the world from the salvation of the world. The truth is that the Bible affirms both the Law 'which worketh wrath' (Rom. iv. 15) and the 'faith which worketh by love' (Gal. v. 6): both Christ's strange work and his proper work."[5]

Bible teacher Warren Wiersbe, in his commentary on Romans, is unequivocal on this passage: "Rulers must bear the sword; that is, they have the power to afflict punishment and even to take life. God established human government because man is a sinner and must have some kind of authority over him. God has given the sword to rulers, and with it the authority to punish and even to execute. Capital punishment was ordained in Genesis 9:5-6, and it has not been abolished. Even though we cannot always respect the man in office, we must respect the office, for government was ordained by God."[6]

Paul himself, though often a victim of the tyranny of Roman rule, declares before the court of Festus: "If then I am a wrongdoer, and have committed anything for which I deserve to die, I do not seek to escape death..." (Acts 25:11). Paul's statement assumes that there are crimes for which the convicted does deserve to die. However, it is essential to note that Paul places very specific emphasis on the responsibility of the public officials to determine the absolute truth of the charges against him. As an agent of God's justice, the state has an immense burden and duty to seek truth. Pontius Pilate was an earthly authority who had to and did understand the weight of this burden to seek justice. When the crowds demanded that Pilate hand Jesus over to be crucified, Pilate symbolically washed his hands in front of them and said: "I am innocent of this man's blood; see to it yourselves" (Matthew 27:24b). Could the crowd possibly have understood the eternal significance of their response: "His blood be on us and on our children" (Matthew 27:25)?

Justice and deterrence

In seeking to examine capital punishment through the lens provided by Scripture, we also need both to remember the sanctity of human life and recognise the image of God in both victim and criminal. Murder is a sin which God punishes with the severity that His perfect justice demands. It is not necessary to regard such punishment as a deterrent at all, but as the only appropriate response to account for one's violation of another's life. Deterrence, as C.S. Lewis argued, is successful if the criminal is deterred, but does not even speak to the issue of justice being done and of consequent rights being upheld. In fact, if deterrence is a factor at all in capital *punishment*, perhaps it is as Anthony Holiday, a professor of philosophy at the University of the Western Cape, puts it: "One person at least is deterred from repeating the capital offence, namely the person executed."

Comments Charles Colson, whose major life work, after his conversion in prison for a Watergate offence as a senior member of the Nixon administration, has been work in prisons with prisoners says this:

> Personally, I still doubt that the death-penalty is a general deterrent – and strong evidence exists that it is not likely to be a deterrent when it is so seldom invoked. But I have a hard time escaping the attitude of the biblical writers, that judgment – both temporal and eschatological – is a *certain* reality for those who disobey or reject God's authority. We'll never know how many potential murderers are deterred by the threat of a death-penalty, just as we will never know how many lives may be saved by it. But at the bare minimum, it may deter a convict sentenced to life from killing a prison guard or another convict. (In such a case no other punishment is appropriate because all lesser punishments have been exhausted.) And it will certainly prevent a convicted murderer from murdering again.[7]

So Scripture does not see capital punishment primarily as a deterrent, nor does it see it primarily as a warning example to others of what will happen to them should they be contemplating murder. This may be troubling for those who call for a return of the death penalty in order that it serve this very purpose. Instead, biblical capital punishment speaks in two directions – with regard to the dignity of the victim, *and* with regard to the humanity of the offender. As Lewis says, "to be punished, however severely, because we have deserved it, because we 'ought to have known better', is to be treated as a human person made in God's image."[8]

Commenting on *The Humanitarian Theory of Punishment* (in his essay of the same title), which says that "the only legitimate motives for punishing are the desire to deter others by example or to mend the criminal", Lewis comments on punishment as "therepeutic" or "palliative", noting,

…it appears at first sight that we have passed from the harsh and self-righteous notion of giving the wicked their deserts to the charitable and enlightened one of tending the psychologically sick. What could be more amiable? …My contention is that this doctrine, merciful though it appears, really means that each one of us, from the moment he breaks the law, is deprived of the rights of a human being.

The reason is this. The Humanitarian theory removes from Punishment the concept of Desert. But the concept of Desert is the only connecting link between punishment and justice. It is only as deserved or undeserved that a sentence can be just or unjust. I do not here contend that the question "Is it deserved?" is the only one we can reasonably ask about a punishment. We may very properly ask whether it is likely to deter others and to reform the criminal. But neither of these two last questions is a question about justice. There is no sense in talking about a "just deterrent" or a "just cure". We demand of a deterrent not whether it is just but whether it will deter. We demand of a cure not whether it is just but whether it succeeds. Thus when we cease to consider what the criminal deserves and consider only what will cure him or deter others, we have tacitly removed him from the sphere of justice altogether; instead of a person, a subject of rights, we now have a mere object, a patient, a "case".[9]

This results in the criminal ceasing to be regarded as a fellow human being with real responsibility for his or her own actions. Instead, the perception is of one who is not a free moral agent – in other words, someone who is less than fully human.

Interestingly enough, it was this essay of C.S. Lewis (*The Humanitarian Theory of Punishment*) which led Charles Colson to change his views on capital punishment to the point where he could say: "I now favour capital punishment, at least in principle, but only in extreme cases when no other punishment can satisfy the demands of justice."

Colson's testimony is instructive. So I am going to let him share it quite fully:

For as long as I can remember, I have opposed capital punishment. As a lawyer I observed how flawed the legal system is, and I concluded, as Justice Learned Hand once remarked, that it was better that a hundred guilty men go free than one innocent man be executed. I was also influenced by very libertarian views of government; I distrusted government too much to give power to take a human life to the judicial system.

Then as I became a Christian, I was confronted with the reality of Jesus' payment of the debt of human sin. I discovered that the operation of God's marvellous grace in our lives has profound implications for the way we live...

The reason for this is quite simple. Justice in God's eyes requires that the response to an offense – whether against God or against humanity – be proportionate. The *lex talionis*, the "law of the talion", served as a restraint, a limitation, that punishment would be no greater than the crime. Yet, implied therein is a standard that the punishment should be *at least as great* as the crime. One frequently finds among Christians the belief that Jesus' so-called "love-ethic" sets aside the "law of the talion." To the contrary, Jesus affirms the divine basis of Old Testament ethics. Nowhere does Jesus set aside the requirements of civil law. Furthermore, it leads to a perversion of legal justice to confuse the sphere of private relations with that of civil law. While the thief on the cross found pardon in the sight of God ("Today you will be with me in Paradise"), that pardon did not extend to eliminating the consequences of his crime ("We are being justly punished, for we are receiving what we deserve for our deeds").

What about mercy? someone is inclined to ask. My response is simple. There can be no mercy where justice is not satisfied. Justice entails receiving what we in fact deserve; we did in fact know better. Mercy is not receiving what we in truth deserve. To be punished, however severely, because we indeed *deserve* it, as C.S. Lewis observed, is to be treated with dignity as human beings created in the image of God. Conversely, to abandon the criteria of righteous and just punishment, as Lewis also pointed out, is to abandon *all* criteria for punishment. Indeed, I am coming to see that mercy extended to offenders whose guilt is certain yet simply ignored creates a moral travesty which, over time, helps pave the way for collapse of the entire social order. This is essentially the argument of Romans 13. Romans 12 concludes with an apostolic proscription of personal retribution, yet St. Paul immediately follows this with a divinely instituted prescription for punishing moral evil. It is for eminently social reasons that "the authorities" are to wield the sword, the *ius gladii*: due to human depravity and the need for moral-social order the civil magistrate punishes criminal behavior. The implication of Romans 13 is that by *not* punishing moral evil the authorities are not performing their God-appointed responsibility in society. Paul's teaching in Romans 13 squares with his personal experience. Testifying before Festus, the Apostle certifies: "If ... I am guilty of doing anything deserving death, I do not refuse to die."[10]

This justice principle is integral to God's character, even as mercy is. But Lewis and Colson would see a divinely instituted tension between mercy and justice – a tension that may not be eradicated. Mercy without justice makes a mockery of the self-sacrifice of the Lamb of God, who makes mercy possible for humans by His own bearing in divine justice the penalty we deserved. For did not God in His justice decree death for sin and then in His mercy pay the penalty Himself in Jesus Christ?

Justice and the justice system

But this principle of just punishment raises another question: will God's wrath not also fall upon a state or system with innocent blood on its hands? It is clear, then, that if the death penalty is a just punishment, it must be administered justly and without any doubt of the truth of the murder conviction. Under the Mosaic Law, for instance, two or three eyewitnesses were necessary in order to secure a conviction for a capital crime. Deuteronomy 19:15 reads: "A single witness shall not prevail against a man for any crime or for any wrong in connection with any offense that he has committed; only on the evidence of two witnesses, or of three witnesses, shall a charge be sustained" (see also Deuteronomy 17:6). Modern convictions, even when made "beyond a reasonable doubt", would rarely be upheld under such standards. For this reason, we must approach such issues of justice with extreme caution. Can a judicial system administer the supreme penalty when its convictions are seldom as certain as our biblical models?

Of course we acknowledge that no justice system can operate with 100 percent accuracy. Mistakes are made. But systems can be put into place to safeguard against mistakes. And there are many examples of this, such as mandatory appeal provisions to the Supreme Court of Appeal when an accused has been sentenced to death.

Jesus Himself provides an example of the self-examination and caution with which we, and our leaders, must approach this responsibility to punish crime. Opponents of capital punishment often cite John 7:53–8:11 as a case in which Jesus rescinds the death penalty prescribed by the Mosaic Law. It is a familiar passage: the Pharisees bring a woman who has been caught in adultery to Jesus, attempting to trap Him with the question "Now in the law Moses commanded us to stone such. What do you say about her?" (John 8:5). Jesus responds: "Let him who is without sin among you be the first to throw a stone at her" (John 8:7). Christ's intention was clearly not to violate the Law of Moses (as the Pharisees hoped he would), but He turned the issue into a question for the accusers instead of the accused. The passage from the Mosaic Law used by the Pharisees to accuse the woman was Deuteronomy 22:22: "If a man is found lying with the wife of another man, both of them shall die, the man who lay with the woman, and the woman; so you shall purge the evil from Israel."

Now, there is no indication in John 8 that the Pharisees intended to punish the man caught in adultery, only that they were using the woman as a tool to trap Jesus. A key point in proper interpretation of Jesus' words in this passage is the meaning of "without sin" (Greek: *anamartetos*). This word appears only once in the New Testament and three times in the Septuagint (the Greek translation of the Hebrew Old Testament). *Anamartetos* was generally used to mean "without fault", but not in the sense of complete sinlessness. Obviously, requiring sinlessness of judges and witnesses would not be consistent with other New Testament passages that affirm human judicial institutions (such as Romans 13). Rather, Jesus was revealing the fault of the Pharisees in failing to uphold consistently all of the provisions of Deuteronomy 22:22. In their judicial proceeding, they were unevenly and unfairly applying the Law against this unnamed woman and not the adulterous man. The inequity and injustice of their administration of capital punishment made the punishment itself morally unacceptable. (We might note, also, in regard to those who would say that, in this passage, Jesus is abolishing the Old Testament provision for the death penalty that adultery, as we discussed above, was not a crime for which God *commanded* a penalty of death; capital punishment was an Old Testament *option* for this offence. Furthermore, it cannot be argued from this passage that Jesus is rescinding the Noahic command to punish murder with death, since the offence here is adultery and not murder.)

We should also register here that the logical conclusion of the argument that Jesus did away with punishment in favour of mercy or the "love ethic" must surely be that it applies evenly across the board to all forms of punishment. But few, I'm sure, would say that all forms imprisonment, for example, should be abolished in favour of mercy.

Self-examination

In light of this biblical model of self-examination, we must cautiously evaluate our own justice system. According to Judge Mark Kumleben, formerly of the appellate division of the Supreme Court of South Africa, one of the great inequalities in a system that permits capital punishment is that some judges will be apt to apply the supreme penalty and some judges will rarely, if ever, sentence the convicted to death. It may be oversimplifying or trivialising the issue to say that avoiding the death sentence in such a system is "the luck of the draw", but unfortunately, the determining factor in many cases may just be the judge's predisposition either for or against capital punishment. In the American West, they used to speak fearfully of "hangin' judges" – those who were especially fond of administering the death penalty. But in a system which allows capital punishment, it is a simple reality: some convicted murderers will be executed though, most will not.

Colson says that, in the United States, "It is merely symbolic justice to execute twenty-five people a year when 2,000 are sentenced."[11] Perhaps more tragic is the fact that factors such a race and socio-economic status may also have a substantial effect on whether an accused murderer is sentenced to death.

Furthermore, economic class, race, and geography are perhaps the best predictors of who will be sentenced to death for first-degree (premeditated) murder. Almost 90 percent of those executed in the U.S. are convicted of killing whites, yet African-Americans and Hispanics are the victims of most homicides. Regarding the African context, I recall reading the account of a former death-row inmate in the apartheid era who remarked with detailed observation that the countries of the African continent, including South Africa, have a poor history in the handling of capital punishment. Politics have too often provided the agenda for judicial process and gruesome abuse has too often frequented the cells and gallows of prisons.

Of course in South Africa at one time the death penalty was "prescribed" for murder, so that the judge's discretion was removed altogether. When he found there were no extenuating circumstances in respect of the murder, he had no choice but to impose the mandatory "prescribed" sentence. Later in South Africa the death penalty as a "prescribed sentence" was abolished and a greater burden was placed on the judges in that it was now within their discretion entirely as to whether or not to impose the death penalty." In the new South African dispensation the death penalty was, of course, to the concern of many, abolished.

A friend who recently retired from his position as a judge in the South African court system remarked that "our society is still very polarised, and judges are inevitably the product of their backgrounds, and that will be true of black judges as much as it's true of white judges. I think one would be naïve to think that every judge from now on is going to be entirely free of inherited preconceptions … and I think that's a very cogent reason not to have the death penalty."[12] With memories of injustice so fresh in our South African psyche, we must proceed with utmost caution. This might not apply to the same degree in Australasia, North America or Europe.

Moral relativism

Further to all this is the fact that our modern societies are permeated with moral relativism. We have seen, in South Africa for example, a transition from one governmental/social authority to another, and the justice system is deemed simply to be a tool of whichever group is in power. C.S. Lewis brings out the point that this kind of reality simply leads to a relativisation of punishments. The death penalty can thus send the message, not that to murder is wrong, but that this present authority, be it black or white, deemed it right that this person should die. However, part of the problem is that, when we call for the death penalty on Scriptural grounds, we do so to a government (or governments) that does not root itself in the same biblical presuppositions. Thus the implementation of capital punishment in such hands can quickly become an exercise in arbitrary notions of what needs "curing" or "deterring". This was illustrated in the apartheid government and still is in many other present governments in Africa and around the world.

Innocent

We can't leave this vexed issue without alluding to the more extreme example of an innocent person executed for a crime he or she did not commit. Many proponents of capital punishment dismiss this difficult problem as an inevitable cost of imposing a just sentence on deserving offenders. However, we recognise that God himself places immense value on every human life, and, as Pontius Pilate would likely warn, innocent blood cannot be merely rinsed off our hands. And it is true that, in systems in which capital punishment is permissible, innocent people are sometimes executed.

Take the United States. It places great value on guaranteeing all accused persons due process of law and actively protecting the rights of the accused. However, the 1992 book, *In Spite of Innocence*, reported that at least twenty-three innocent people were executed there in the last century. And in the twenty-five years before 1992, sixty-nine Americans awaiting execution were released from death row, not so much because it was proven they had been falsely convicted, but because there was shown to be sufficient doubt in the conviction as to justify setting aside the death penalty.

Clearly any court system has to safeguard itself profoundly from any miscarriages of justice. The first step is to inspect the integrity and fairness of the system, before entrusting it with the monumental responsibility of administering the supreme penalty.

A continuing discussion

And so, it seems, we end back at the beginning. God so values humanity, made in His image, that the shedding of innocent blood is a most serious offence against Him. For this reason, Scripture allows the state to punish this sin with the supreme penalty on earth. But, for the same reason, we must ensure that our justice system has the integrity necessary to bear this responsibility before we reinstate capital punishment. God detests hands that shed innocent blood, be they the hands of a murderer on the street, or a state that executes an innocent person.

And Scripture does not just leave its discussion of the sanctity of human life at the question of capital punishment. Issues of justice of all kinds – sexual, economic, social, etc. – are all central to the holiness code as found in Leviticus 17–26. To believe in the sanctity of human life is not simply to punish its violation, but to exalt it with appropriately just and compassionate personal behaviour, family conduct and societal laws and institutions. And to tackle the root of the violation of life, one tackles sin. The process for that obviously lies in the church's mandate to serve the world with a life of servanthood and holiness, seeking to "make disciples of all nations … teaching them to observe everything I [Jesus] have commanded you" (Matthew 28:19-20). Thus the only deterrence the Bible finally speaks of is that which comes through the Gospel, heard and seen in the mouths and actions of us, Christ's servants to the world. And the power of the Gospel manifests itself in the transformation of both individual and community through the forgiveness of sins and reconciliation with Jesus Christ as Lord and Saviour.

We must not forget, as we continue this discussion, as both church and nation, that our God is holy and just. And when He entrusts human institutions with the privilege and responsibility of acting as agents of His justice, He gives a challenge which must be approached with honesty and self-examination.

This is a discussion to be continued in my own country, as in many others. However, my own posture is that I would like to see the death penalty on our statue books as the *poena suprema* which criminals would fear. But, because of past abuses, it should be hedged round with such tight foolproof provisos (for example, the two or three witnesses of Old Testament specification) so that its use was very rare.

"Where the state considers the life of a deliberate murderer to have greater value than the life of an innocent victim, it demeans the *imago Dei* in mankind and weakens the supports of social justice."[13]

My own feelings are well captured by Charles Colson's testimony:

> In spite of my misgivings, I've come to see capital punishment as an essential element of justice. On the whole, the full range of biblical data weighs in its favour. Society should not execute capital offenders merely for the sake of revenge, rather to balance the scales of moral justice which have been disturbed. The death-penalty is warranted and should be implemented *only* in those cases where evidence is certain, in accordance with the biblical standard and where no other punishment can satisfy the demands of justice.
>
> In the public debate over the death-penalty, we are dealing with values of the highest order: respect for the sacredness of human life and its protection, the preservation of order in society, and the attainment of justice through law."[14]

End Notes

1. John Murray, *The Epistle to the Romans – The English Text with Introduction, Exposition and Notes, Vol. 2* (Grand Rapids, Michigan: William B. Eerdmans Publishing Co., 1965), 152-153.

2. Murray, 153.

3. William Sanday and Arthur Headlam, *The Epistle to the Romans – A Critical and Exegetical Commentary* (Edinburgh: T. & T. Clark, 1895), 367-368.

4. Sanday and Headlam, 368.

5. F.F. Bruce, *The Epistle of Paul to the Romans – An Introduction and Commentary* (London: Tyndale Press, 1963), 238.

6. Warren W. Wiersbe, *Be Right* (Amersham-on-the-Hill, England: Scripture Press Foundation U.K. Ltd., 1987), 153.

7. Charles Colson, "Capital Punishment: A Personal Statement", Prison Fellowship, <http://www.pfm.org/AM/Template. cfm?Section=Issues_and_Research1&TEMPLATE=/CM/ ContentDisplay.cfm&CONTENTID=2252>, March 3, 2006.

8. C.S. Lewis, "The Humanitarian Theory of Punishment", *Compelling Reason – Essays on Ethics and Theology*, Walter Hooper, ed. (London: HarperCollins Publishers, 1996), 133. Comments Hooper: "Of all Lewis' essays, this is one of the most respected and one of the most controversial" (End notes, p. 185).

9. Lewis, 128.

10. Colson, "Capital Punishment: A Personal Statement."

11. Colson, "Capital Punishment: A Personal Statement."

12. Letter to the author from Judge Mark Kumleben, 1995.

13. Carl F.H. Henry, "Perspectives on Capital Punishment", *Twilight of a Great Civilization* (Westchester, Illinois: Crossway Books, 1988), 71.

14. Colson, "Capital Punishment: A Personal Statement."

Chapter Ten

PROSPERITY, POVERTY AND *SHALOM* – SOME THOUGHTS ON A THEOLOGY OF MONEY

A decade ago, a South African businessman asked a colleague if he knew how to get a small business in South Africa. Seeing his friend's bewildered look, he duly provided the answer, "First buy a big one, and soon it will be a small one!" Said a father to a colleague, "If you want to teach your children the value of the Rand, you had better do it quickly!" Thankfully, some of these sad economic realities are changing.

Actually, if one thinks a conversation anywhere about money is a complicated business, just try it in South Africa. I am glad that economists in post-apartheid South Africa can indeed point to significant growth (4 percent), but at the same time more and more people are unable to find jobs, or are losing jobs or are looking overseas for better jobs. In South Africa, of course, money has a particular history in the apartheid background. Through despotic administration of land, resources and people, apartheid led to our nation possessing a First World infrastructure primarily uplifting less than 20 percent of the population and leaving the other 80 percent at Third World standards. This means that in this country, money, prosperity and poverty come deeply loaded with the complicating factor of race. While somewhat less true now, it is still a general reality that a discussion of money and poverty in South Africa cannot, at least at this stage, be divorced from issues of race, reconciliation, and right relationships at all levels, including the economic one.

This is where the Old Testament notion of *shalom* comes in, *shalom* being that state of peace where everything and everyone is operating in right relationships under God – i.e., humans to God, spouse to spouse, parents to children, citizens to state and vice versa, people to environment, individuals to their work and money, etc. Where all those realities are in right, God-ordained relationships with each other, there is *shalom*.

Debunking some myths on poverty and prosperity

Myth 1: *The poor are under judgement*

Here and there is a faddish Christian concept of the poor which regards their state as a form of divine judgment and conversely sees prosperity as sure proof of God's blessing. It must be said that from a biblical perspective there is no truth at all in the first concept and only an element of truth in the second.

In a whopping 197 references to the word "poor/poverty" in the NIV Bible, not a single verse condemns those who are poor. Less than a dozen verses are warnings that certain actions will lead to poverty. In other words, poverty is not a sin, though how one becomes poor may at times involve sin, e.g., laziness and indulgence. In fact, the vast majority of verses about the poor both lament their plight and command compassionate actions towards them. These verses further condemn oppression and the exploitation of the poor.

Myth 2: *Prosperity is never a sign of God's blessing*

While we do not agree with the excesses of the Prosperity Gospel, we can nevertheless affirm firstly that poverty is a quality of life that is wholly contrary to God's intentions for humanity and therefore unacceptable, and secondly, that prosperity is indeed often, but not always, celebrated in Scripture as indicative of divine blessing. The book of Deuteronomy, which fleshes out God's covenant relationship with Israel, is full of teaching reflecting God's intention for all to live an abundant life (Deuteronomy 28:9-12). This thinking goes back to Genesis 2, in Eden, where humanity lives in harmonious relationship with God and creation, and consequently experiences the richness of all that creation has to offer. In other words, wherever people are living in submission to the Lord, they will experience the blessings of His rule in their lives.

Myth 3: *Prosperity is always a sign of God's blessing*

Actually, in Scripture we see that far from prosperity always being a sign of blessing, it is all too often the possession, not of the blessed, but of wicked exploiters, who have obtained it at the expense of the poor. The psalmist complained, "For I was envious of the arrogant, when I saw the prosperity of the wicked ... always at ease, they increase in riches" (Psalm 73:3,12). Scripture also shows that wealth can come by many means, whether by hard work, God's blessing, or exploitation, fraud, and even theft.

Myth 4: We can serve both God and money
This is impossible! The Scriptures say wealth can all too quickly become our god. Jesus warned of this when in Matthew 6:24 he said, "you cannot serve God and mammon". Christian writer Richard Foster's personal testimony, in his classic book, *The Challenge of the Disciplined Life: Christian reflections on money, sex and power*, is that, "The thing I failed to see, and the thing that Jesus saw so clearly, is the way in which mammon makes a bid for our hearts."[1] Wealth can indeed become our god, and often does. This is easy to see when we examine our choices and priorities and find what really controls our lives.

Freed of our mythologies, we must ask what the truth is about the poor and their relationship to wealth. We think first not of ideals, but of realities.

Some realities of poverty and wealth in the world in which we live

A global view
This is necessary because what South Africa, for example, experiences is not unique, and global trends help inform us of some basic realities about poverty. A free market economy (i.e., an economic system in which any person in the private sector is free to participate with minimal government controls on market mechanisms) dominates the global market. It might be inferred from this that an individual's own economic behaviour or habits will decide his or her material well-being. But a mitigating factor is that there are power structures in the global economy, ultimately located in the hands of a few, mainly Western, nations and institutions, which exert huge controls in global economic exchanges that obviously favour themselves. Most know the "trickle-down" theory in global macroeconomics which says the profits gained by the capable and well-placed will inevitably trickle beneficially down to the underprivileged or marginalised.

There is little evidence, though, that such an effect inevitably works. Statistically this is seen in the fact that a fifth of the world's population receives more than four-fifths of the world's income. According to a World Bank report, not so long ago 1.3 billion people in the developing world still struggle to survive on less than $1 a day and the number continually increases. Ouch! All this underlines that one cause of poverty is found in localised consequences of a globalised free market economy. There is little or nothing a poor person, community or nation is able to do about this. This challenges the Christian conscience.

A historical view

People are often poor because events of history have brought them to that point. There is no need to elaborate on some of the exploitations and their consequences in colonialism, or the fruits of apartheid in my own country, for example, except to say that a loss of spirit and motivation in certain of our communities right now cannot be so much attributed to laziness as to the near destruction of their social cohesion and structures by apartheid laws.

South African poor, especially the victims of apartheid, are accordingly on a journey of social, cultural and economic repair that could take generations. This recovery is essential to their social well-being, economic participation and success.

A sociological view: the spiral of poverty

Sometimes a combination of wretched factors can intersect and feed a debilitating spiral of poverty, where the poor, frequently a black or brown person, is often trapped in a poverty spiral generally hard for whites to understand. In South Africa this poverty spiral is desperate, with one calamitous consequence following almost inevitably upon another.

First, economic and political exploitation beget poverty, which spawns in turn more children, more overcrowding, more poor hygiene, more disease and higher infant mortality. Following a consequent lowering of morale and motivation, the spiral continues with population growth exceeding affordable and healthy food, leading to even more poverty, more malnutrition, and yet more infant mortality.

All this causes retarded physical and intellectual growth in young survivors, plus decreased potential for academic and other achievement, and finally in yet more ignorance, the latter feeding both poor work performance and finally unemployment. In light of all this, how do Christians respond?

How do we as Christians respond to issues of wealth and poverty?

A Christian analysis of this problem gets us nowhere if it is not accompanied by a proactive response. The Kingdom of God, as the Bible calls it, is the arena of solutions, healing, redemption and restoration through Jesus Christ to a whole and healthy existence, where *shalom* has a chance to prevail. What is key to *shalom*, however, is not simply that it comes from God's loving rule, but that it exists wherever communities are living in obedience to His rule and therefore reflecting the ways of His kingdom.

Insofar as money is concerned, what does it mean to be in *shalom* and obedient to the demands of Jesus?

Shalom *means everyone giving, supplying the needs of others and knowing the blessings of it*

Few promises in Scripture are more dramatic than Malachi 3:10. Here we are literally challenged by God with the principle of giving one tenth of our material resources directly to Him and His work. Listen to the familiar text: "'Bring the full tithes into the storehouse, that there may be food in my house; and thereby put me to the test,' says the Lord of hosts, 'if I will not open the windows of heaven for you and pour down for you an overflowing blessing.'"

I have never, ever known anyone anywhere who tithed faithfully, even out of poverty, who did not have a ringing testimony to the miraculous and faithful financial or material provision of God. He opens the windows of heaven and the consequent blessings are astonishing, not making us rich, but providing adequacy. To me it is an endless mystery why believers try to avoid tithing or ministers try to avoid teaching it. True, we are not under law but under grace, but if believers tithed under the law, then under grace "cheerful givers" (2 Corinthians 9:7) of the New Testament will want to make the Old Testament requirement the minimal starting point for giving. And they will then inherit in blessing the even more remarkable New Testament equivalent of the Malachi 3:10 promise, "And God is able to provide you with every blessing in abundance, so that you may always have enough of everything and may provide in abundance for every good work" (2 Corinthians 9:8). And note the thanksgiving of Paul for the Macedonians where even "their extreme poverty have overflowed in a wealth of liberality on their part" as they gave "beyond their means" (2 Corinthians 8:2-3).

Actually, to the extent that we wrestle against giving away our money, particularly the tithe mandated in the Old Testament – to that extent we admit both that money is our god and faithlessness our sad condition. When it is difficult to summon the will to give, we must ask ourselves the question whether we see our final security residing in Christ or in our finances.

We should also add that giving should not be a matter of careless, thoughtless or directionless handouts. We are called to steward prayerfully the gifts we have received (Matthew 25:14-30). God's Spirit must then guide and "Each one must do as he has made up his mind, not reluctantly or under compulsion" (2 Corinthians 9:7).

One interesting observation in all this was underlined afresh to me in 2005 when our African Enterprise team conducted two missions, one to leadership and another more generally to the whole city of Antananarivo, capital of Madagascar. It is a city fraught with desperate poverty. A pastor there called Jules told me after I had preached with him among some desperately poor people that his now very big and flourishing congregation had been mainly built out of the ranks of the very poor. I asked Pastor Jules, seeing so many of his people had been won initially in open-air street meetings, whether he found that there was an economic and social upliftment once they were converted to Christ.

You see, being in the middle of all this poverty reminded me of a discussion I had many years ago with the late Bishop Stephen

Neill about the big debate then going on in the World Council of Churches about whether amongst the poor, Humanisation and Social Action always had to precede Redemption and Gospel Proclamation. I remember Stephen Neill saying, even as one deeply involved in World Council of Churches activities at that time, that he took strong issue with the WCC's philosophy on that point because it was so often used as an excuse and fig-leaf for not preaching the Gospel of the Cross and conversion to the poor because one felt guilty in doing so without having worked on the practical side of social upliftment.

Bishop Neill said that in India many poor people were launched on the process of economic and social upliftment by conversion itself. This he had discovered after 42 years of missionary work in India. So now I was putting the same question to Pastor Jules. Did social upliftment and economic improvement take place in the lives of the poor after they were converted?

"Definitely", said Jules. "Many of the thousands of people in my congregations came from the poorest of the poor and many even were beggars. Today they are well off and even driving 4x4s! The key", he said, "is thoroughly discipling them in the ways of the Lord and from day one teaching tithing, regardless of how poor they are. Even if the tithe is only 2 or 3 cents, they should give it. Then as they do so, the miracle of Malachi 3:10 begins to kick in miraculously as the Lord proceeds to "open the windows of heaven for you and pour down for you an overflowing blessing." Jules added that probably the most generous and greatest givers in his church were people who had come from the poorest of the poor, but now they were generous and often even lavish givers. Of course it is also true that once people are truly converted they stop wasting the little money they have on drink, womanising, cigarettes, or gambling. They also start to keep their houses clean, even if they are very poor and this starts to eliminate disease and the unhealthy environment.

May I add before leaving this my own view that no one is fully converted to Christ until their pocketbook is fully converted! That said, we do need to register also that love needs to be built in to our economic and political structures.

Shalom *means love built into both economic and political structures*

Justice, in my view, whether political or economic, is simply love built into structures. This means that in every way available to us, we should be working for an economic system of love and justice which takes seriously that material adequacy and absence of scarcity are basic to human well-being. Love knows this. So does justice. This puts two major challenges before economic thinkers, especially in places like South Africa, about how to share the cake more fairly and how to expand it more vigorously so that more people might benefit, especially the poor and marginalised.

Some years ago Professor James Moulder of the University of KwaZulu-Natal published an instructive article on this, calling for a shifting of the goalposts in the debate between capitalism and socialism. He noted that "we cannot have a free enterprise system that does not generate inequality and poverty [and we] cannot have an egalitarian system that is not restrictive and frustrating." Instead, Moulder calls us to a paradigm shift involving three rules. The first says that it is always legitimate to ask how we can increase the productivity and wealth of an organisation or society. The second says that it is always legitimate to ask how we can distribute the profits and wealth of an organisation or society more fairly. The third says that it is never legitimate to ask the first question (the one about productivity and wealth) without asking the second question (the one about distribution and fairness). And the other way round.

Moulder sees rule three as crucial, meaning that, "anyone who wants to increase wealth must tell us how to distribute it more fairly, [while] anyone who wants to distribute wealth more fairly must tell us how to generate it more effectively and efficiently."[2] As we move more into the realm of Christian principle, the result should lead us to a creative form of mixed economy geared specially to the needs of our nations at this time. Another great need in all situations is to provide somehow a safety net beneath the unemployed.

Shalom *does mean a deep concern for the poor*

It is clear throughout Scripture that God's attitude to the poor is identical to His attitude toward other kinds of oppressed groupings. Now although Scripture speaks of the poor in three senses – the economically poor (those with little money), the politically poor (those suffering powerlessly as victims of social injustice) and the spiritually poor (those who are humble, meek and spiritually hungry) – it remains so that Jesus spent much of His time with the poor peasants of Galilee, the literal poor, and had a great affinity for all those at the bottom of the heap. Indeed, He Himself was one of them and often had "nowhere to lay his head" (Matthew 8:20). Small wonder then that Jesus, in Matthew 25:44-45, could finish His parable of the sheep and the goats by saying, "Then they also will answer, 'Lord, when did we see thee hungry or thirsty or a stranger or naked or sick or in prison, and did not minister to thee?' Then he will answer them, 'Truly, I say to you, as you did it not to one of the least of these, you did it not to me.'"

Now what we have to grasp, difficult as we may find it, is that this concern for the poor and needy is to permeate our social behaviour and call forth a compassionate and generous servant attitude towards all who find themselves on the "underneath" side of life, even when it is the result of their own mistakes or, in some cases, ineptitude. And even more so when it results from exploitation by the rich and powerful. Indeed the Scriptures abound with intense denunciation of those who exploit the poor. For example, in Ezekiel 22, blazing divine condemnation rests on a catalogue of sins in which "extortion" (vv. 7,12) and "dishonest gain"(v. 13) which are "destroying lives" (v. 27) are set as equally serious alongside murder and idolatry (vv. 3-4), "contempt" for parents (v. 7), lewd acts (v. 9), and adultery and incest (v. 11).

In this regard, the Anglican Lambeth Conference of bishops in 1998 was right, and operating in the spirit of Scripture, when it called on Western financial powers to consider seriously the cancellation of Third World debts. Thus Lambeth Resolution I:15, while thankful for what some political and financial leaders were doing, went further and said: "The need for debt relief for the poorest nations is urgent. Children are dying and societies are unravelling under the burden of debt. We call for negotiations to be speeded up so that the poorest nations may benefit from such cancellation by the birth of the new millennium."[3] That shows a deep concern for the poor. It is an example for all of us.

Conclusion

The issues, as we have seen, are massive and complex, often at both a personal micro level and certainly at a macro one. But this is a truly major issue at many levels now in our millennium. As we said earlier, if one fifth of the world enjoys 85 percent of its income, and 1.3 billion people in the developing world struggle to survive on less than $1 a day, then the Christian Church dare not turn its back on this monumental challenge under God.

And in my own country of South Africa in particular, given our apartheid history and our present racial issues, with the consequent divide of rich and poor (often, but thankfully not always, along racial lines) in our nation, reconciliation is a priority, even in economics! The Christian would also insist that the reconciliation of rich and poor, wherever they are, as well as of other alienated groupings, will only happen with reconciliation in Jesus Christ as its basis and departure point.

In the meantime, each of us faces our own money and our own Lord. In this regard I leave you with two sound dicta. The first from John Wesley: "Make all you can. Save all you can. Give all you can." The second is from John Calvin: "The only right stewardship of money is that which is tested by the rule of love."

End Notes

1. Richard Foster, *The Challenge of the Disciplined Life: Christian reflections on money, sex and power* (San Francisco: HarperSanFrancisco, 1989), 26.
2. James Moulder, "Comparing Oranges with Apples", *The Natal Witness* (June 29, 1989). For a fuller discussion of this see Chapter 14 on *Structural Sharing* in my book *The Politics of Love*, Michael Cassidy – see Chapter 14 on "Structural Planning", Hodder & Stoughton, London, 1991, 211-231.
3. Lambeth Conference 1998 – Section I Resolutions, <http://www.anglicancommunion.org/lambeth/1/sect1rpt.html>, March 3, 2006.

Chapter Eleven

SIX DAYS SHALT THOU DO SOMETHING
OR OTHER: A THEOLOGY OF WORK

Note that the flip slide of the Fourth Commandment on keeping
the Sabbath day holy says: "Six days you shall labour, and do all
your work" (Exodus 20:9) – not all your something or other!
"Work for six days? Dreadful thought", moans one. "Work for
six days?" says the workaholic, "What a pleasure – make it
seven!" "Work for six days?" says the unemployed, "Oh God,
just give me work, any work, for one day, or six, or seven. I am
soul-destroyed for lack of work." "I love my work", says the
missionary doctor.

The above responses to this principle in the Fourth
Commandment indicate an assortment of views and experiences
of work, revealing that all of us probably get this critical
component of life wrong at some point or other. The fact is that
we are all in a relationship with work – whether it be joyous,
obsessive, stressful or grievous – and whether we handle it with
diligence, laziness, delight or resentment. All the more reason to
seek the relationship with it which the Bible desires for us.

In the beginning was work

God the worker
In the creation narrative of Genesis 1–2:4 we see God the worker
who worked six days, found it "good" and rested on the seventh.
There was also revelation, light, order, meaning and purpose in
God's work, which itself was an incredible expression of His
character and intentions. Creation was the work and expression
of a love that must produce.

People as workers
In chapters 1–2 of Genesis we see that man and woman are
also created, not just as happy companions to each other, but
as workers. Says Genesis 2:8,15, "And the Lord God planted a
garden in Eden... The Lord God took the man and put him in

the garden of Eden to till it and keep it." Indeed, the work Adam and Eve carried out was reflective of their human identity as being made in the image of God. Reflecting God to creation, they were to nurture, tend, steward, care, and effect godly, righteous rule over all the earth. Even when the fall took place, Adam and Eve were still mandated to carry out the work to which God had originally called them in being fruitful, multiplying, and working the land. Although work would now be painful and toilsome as well – the consequences of our disobedience impacting on our entire existence – work was still the blessing it was intended to be (Genesis 3:16-19). Our work is glorifying to God. So here is God the worker with His people as workers alongside Him and together managing the divine creation. And from then on work becomes integral to living – something we live to do, not something we do to live. Work is the heartbeat of our existence under God, and the sacred dynamic of living.

Work as dignity

A major implication of the creation narrative is the dignity of work. This principle must apply to the work we are in, or are planning, or which we give to others. And indeed even Jesus, before He went about His Father's redemptive work, worked manually at a carpenter's bench, where His work had dignity no less than that of the lawyers, merchants or bureaucrats of His time.

But sadly we all know only too well that for many people their work is monotonous, dreary, even soul-destroying and void of any worthy challenge. By contrast, the Genesis narrative and other Scriptures would imply that employers should be seeking for their workers and themselves real job fulfilment in the workplace and the elimination of destructive monotony. People should also grasp where their contribution fits in the overall scheme of things. When two medieval stonemasons were once questioned as to what they were doing, one said, "I am laying some bricks." Said the other: "I am building a cathedral." For the first worker, his work lacked the dignity and meaning which the second had found because he could see where his contribution fitted in the overall scheme of things.

Work as worship

To work responsibly and within the parameters God has set is to bring honour to Him and demonstrate our love for Him. In fact, our primary motivation in work should be to serve God. In the 17th Century, Brother Lawrence, a kitchen hand in a monastery, learned that worship can lie at the heart of even the most menial of tasks. His work of washing dishes to the glory of God led him to write the devotional classic, *Practising the Presence of God*. Over her kitchen sink at home, Billy Graham's wife, Ruth, always had a sign, "Divine service held here three times daily"! A New York shoeshine boy said he shone every pair of shoes, "as if they were on Jesus' feet!" Presenting ourselves – and that includes our work – to the living God is our "spiritual act of worship" (Romans 12:1 – NIV).

Work as service

Work is also about serving our fellow human beings, and not just ourselves. The second of two commands in Jesus' summary of the entire will of God was to "love your neighbour as yourself" (Matthew 22:39). In fact there are few joys greater in life than those occasional moments when we suddenly realise we have completely forgotten ourselves in the service of someone, and joy, in consequence, has entered our souls. And what a blessing for any and all if their work can be interpreted and experienced as a service to others in the Name of the Lord!

Work as idolatry

Work as an act of worship and service can also readily be perverted into idolatry when it not only defines who we are, but obsessively consumes all our energies and all our available time, seven days a week, 24 hours a day. In this case we cease to be "called" people and become driven ones. A monkey is on our back until finally we see that, "Better is a handful of quietness than two hands full of toil and a striving after wind" (Ecclesiastes 4:6). Listen further to Solomon speaking on the workaholic businessman who finally comes to his senses: "Again, I saw vanity under the sun: a person who has no one, either son or brother, yet there is no end to all his toil, and his eyes are never satisfied with riches, so that he never asks, 'For whom am I toiling and depriving myself of pleasure?' This also is vanity and an unhappy business" (Ecclesiastes 4:7-8). In fact, work becomes something degraded when it becomes either oppressive or obsessive and when it is done outside the will or ways or word of the Lord.

The ease with which humanity perverts work from worship to idolatry and from dignity to degradation has one key antidote called rest. In an age of nervous exhaustion, burnout and absence of margin amongst millions, this is a key notion.

The necessity of rest
Scripture advances at least three reasons for this rest:

God rested, so all must rest
In Genesis 2:3, after six days of creation, God rested from His work. Not because He was tired and not because it was high time for some inactivity, for Scripture says God is working actively in history up to this day (John 5:16). Rather, He rested because His work of creation was complete and therefore in a state of restfulness. This is the foundation point for the Biblical practice of the Sabbath – a practice so radical in scope and implication, that to implement it on a widespread basis today would send shockwaves through society and ironically, would send many businesses into a frenzy.

So out of this the Old Testament teaches that everything – people, animals, land – and everyone needs regular occasions to rest (literally, to be "released"). And God himself points the way.

Resting shows we honour God as finally in charge
When we rest we also honour God as the one who finally controls our lives and is in the end the one who grants or withholds fruitfulness and who enables or inhibits prosperity. After all, Jesus is finally in charge, being the one in whom "all things were created" and in whom "all things hold together" (Colossians 1:16-17). So when we take a break, the God who "will neither slumber nor sleep" (Psalm 121:4) stays on the job! In fact, when Israel was commanded to give themselves and their land a rest on every seventh day for a day, and on every seventh year for a year, it was in order to remember that behind creation's

fruitfulness and their well-being was God, not primarily their own hard work. So the surgeon can rest at some point as God picks up His healing role in cooperative work with His servant, the surgeon.

Likewise the farmer may plant and sow, but God finally is the one who brings forth the harvest. God's words to the farmer are powerful, "the land is mine ... you are merely my tenants..." (Leviticus 25:23 – The Living Bible). Leaving the land to rest for an entire year and ceasing from labour during that time would surely test the farmer's faith in God's sustaining grace! Yet the Lord asked exactly that of his Old Testament people for their land's good and ultimately for their own.

Resting prevents us damaging ourselves

Israel's Sabbath laws also affirmed that to work without rest is to abuse and damage our resources, ourselves, and those around us who also depend on those resources. Indeed, how often when we do set aside time for Sabbath worship and rest, do we realise how immeasurably the pause, the refreshment and the opportunity for reflection have benefited us? We even find it radically altering our perspectives on priorities, and energising us in new ways for work yet to come. I believe multitudes today are suffering at many levels – health, family, mental, emotional, etc. – from failure to "keep Sunday special" and once a week take a proper rest break. Even a casual reader of the Old Testament will know what weight is put on the Sabbath principle (Exodus 20:8, 31:16, Deuteronomy 5:12, Isaiah 58:13). In fact, listed often in Old Testament catalogues of sin is "profaning the Sabbath" (e.g., Nehemiah 13:17, Ezekiel 23:38). Even the unlikely Voltaire could say: "If you want to kill Christianity, you must abolish Sunday." But more than that, if we want to kill ourselves, we must abolish Sunday. It is there for worship, spiritual renewal, restoration, recreation and physical rest, and we ignore this special gift and mandate at our peril. And for the minister who works on Sunday, let there be a sacrosanct day off somewhere in the week, plus proper and adequate annual leave, along with the midweek equivalent of an occasional weekend away.

Ethics and work

Godly conduct required in the workplace

Scripture's call for holy living also means a call for ethical conduct in the workplace as rooted in the holy character of God. To be unethical in the workplace is to violate the laws of righteousness and justice that God has built into His creation. Scripture is full of warnings against injustices in the workplace. Leviticus19:13-14 forbids both fraud and holding back from workers what they are due, whether in wages, recognition, or appropriate benefits, time off etc. And there are divinely ordained consequences to our conduct! Any, be it bosses, companies or other institutions who exploit the poor or favour the rich to get rich, are actually bringing themselves by natural cause and effect to ruin (see Proverbs 22:16 and 28:3, 8). And Ezekiel 18:5-9 shows that the one who conducts himself righteously, including in his business conduct, will live. If he does not, he will die (v. 13)!

Integrity required

Scripture also calls us to integrity – i.e., honesty in detail – in our workplace. Proverbs 20:23 says, referring to the means of economic exchange of that day, "Diverse weights are an abomination to the Lord, and false scales are not good." Leviticus 19:35-36 echoes this sentiment by explicitly forbidding any form of deception or hidden adjustment in economic transactions. Besides, Scripture would see anything unjust as ultimately inefficient economically, and anything just as ultimately efficient, regardless of first impressions.

Godly attitudes required

Scripture also calls us to godly attitudes in the workplace. Working peaceably with all people (Romans 12:18), having a servant heart (Matthew 20:26), and bearing ourselves with humility (Philippians 2:3-7), are all aspects of a godly work ethic. Ultimately, we are to bring to our job what it means to be a disciple of Jesus Christ. The arduous aim before us, at which of course we fail much, is to reflect His character in every detail of life and work. One helpful suggestion is to read through Paul's list of the fruit of the Spirit (Galatians 5:22-24), concentrating on one at a time – perhaps for a week at a time – keeping it before us at work, praying for the Spirit to bring it into greater reality in our working life.

Excellence also required

Finally, Scripture calls us to diligence and excellence in the workplace. Proverbs rebukes the lazy, saying: "He who is slack in his work is a brother to him who destroys" (18:9), and "The desire of the sluggard kills him for his hands refuse to labor" (21:25)! On the other hand, disciplined work habits lead not just to sufficiency (13:11), but to reward: "Do you see a man skilful in his work? He will stand before kings; he will not stand before obscure men" (22:29). In any event, "Whatever your task, work heartily, as serving the Lord and not men" (Colossians 3:23).

A word to those without work

Deep compassion and concern are required for many who are currently unemployed and for whom the task of finding work has become an oppressive burden in itself. They know unemployment for the curse that it is. However, to any without work in the formal sense of the word, the Lord still brings a word of comfort in affirming that their very lives and conduct are seen by Him as an arena of His ongoing activity and grace. Here spiritual and other lessons can be learned which are not learnable in the regular context of normal employment. To such we say that, while God knows you need work and an income in order to make a living, His faithful eye is nevertheless on you and on your material needs even more than for the sparrow or the flowers of the field (Matthew 6:25-34). Indeed, no circumstance, however seemingly hopeless, is void of potential for the one who is creator of the universe. And Christ promises to those who abide in Him that they will know His faithfulness in their lives

While the wilderness of unemployment which some are in seems barren of hope, nevertheless such a person, while proactively seeking work or developing new skills for the workplace and praying for job opportunities, may at a personal level be like a tree planted by streams of water, which even "in the year of drought [e.g., unemployment] … does not cease to bear fruit" (Jeremiah 17:8). Let this principle from Jeremiah encourage any in the dark times (hopefully only temporary) of unemployment, knowing that Christ is as in control of this season of your life as He has been in sovereign control of others – or indeed of the seasons of the world.

A word to those who know those without work

Statistics about available, viable and long-term employment show that a person does not have to be lazy to be without work. Unemployment is rife, for example, in South Africa, with recent estimates putting it between 33 percent and 40 percent. Others put it higher. This is a deeply discouraging and debilitating place for many of our people to be in. Regardless of how stable or industrious a person is, to be caught in the cycle of unemployment stabs the heart with messages of worthlessness, rejection, divine disinterest or even divine powerlessness. What such people need from those of us who do have work is not a patronising exhortation to try harder, or a pat on the back with an assurance that it will all work out in the end, but rather our practical assistance in their need. This may be financial, or helping them learn a skill or how to understand the job market, or supporting them in training, and especially being their friends and companions in what can be a lonely, alienating experience of life, until the new day of proper employment dawns with healing in its wings.

Conclusion

Celebration and creativity, worship and service, diligence and restfulness, industry and leisure, compassion and justice, honesty and integrity – all these things are key components in the challenging mechanisms and meanings of work as seen in the Scriptures. For these to be discovered in all our countries by all in our potential workforces means that all – whether in government or private sector or labour or management or even the Church – need to labour to ensure a growing economy with an economic system by which wealth is not only generated but also shared. We also have to say that, in places like South Africa, shattering, debilitating strikes and work stoppages by labour unions will in all likelihood not help to make us competitive or maximally productive as a nation. Beyond that they could well accelerate rather than diminish the curse of unemployment, and put beyond reach the 6 percent growth rate necessary to provide work and jobs for all coming into the South African work market.

And of course these principles apply equally to Australia, Europe, North America or anywhere else.

As for Mr and Mrs Citizen, especially the Lord's citizens wherever they are, we all have to work to find God's best way for us in our work, above all doing whatever we do to "work heartily, as serving the Lord" (Colossians 3:22) and seeking "first his kingdom and his righteousness", knowing that as we do this, all other things will be given to us "as well" (Matthew 6:33), including meaningful work.

Chapter Twelve

WHAT ON EARTH ARE YOU DOING FOR HEAVEN'S SAKE?

THE ENVIRONMENT, CREATION AND THE BIBLE

Time magazine not so long ago dedicated a special issue to the subject of the environment, and placed these words on the front cover: "Why saving the environment will be the next century's biggest challenge."[1] And, indeed, many Christian thinkers also believe that the greatest threat to the human race at the opening of the 21st century is not a wartime but a peacetime peril – namely the ruination of our planet's natural resources and delicate ecosystems by crude exploitation and mindless greed.

Let us reflect for a moment on just how glorious God's creation is, and we may understand the gravity of such statements. The Psalmist proclaims: "When I consider your heavens, the work of your fingers, the moon and the stars, which you have set in place, what is man that you are mindful of him, the son of man that you care for him?" (Psalm 8:3-4 – NIV).

Also instructive in the creation story is the fact that after each day's creation, God paused and saw "that it was *good*". It is a short phrase, but power-packed.

Praise of nature is, of course, not limited to the Bible nor to Christian writings. Endless volumes overflow in poem and prose about nature. But in my view only supernaturalists really see nature because only they see the signature of God that sets it all ablaze with meaning. In fact, says both the Bible and experience, all creation is one giant system of interdependence – grass upon soil, animals upon grass, humans upon animals, fish upon sea, birds upon air and all of us upon God.

Humanly, of course, we also live from each other and for each other. That is why self-sufficiency is the outrage of creation, and the loss of community, a wounding blow to God's creative purposes for us. Likewise, the loss of human care for the divine handiwork. Even more of an outrage is to be humanly deaf to the speech of God in creation.

If beyond that, we believe there is no God in creation to speak, we are not only left with no explanation for ourselves, as minds amidst the mindless, souls amidst the soulless, and personality amidst the impersonal, but we also become cosmic orphans lost in a cosmic farce. We are the children of chance, isolated, lonely and friendless in a friendless universe – a universe we know a lot about, but which belongs to no one. And the mystery of existence overwhelms us. So, that is where we end up unless we start with "In the beginning God …" (Genesis 1:1).

Causes for concern

It should be self-evident that creation and the environment are immensely precious to us humans as our terrestrial dwelling place in space. Yet we are curiously poor stewards and housekeepers of our planet. That being so, it is obvious how essential it is for a Christian to be able to think rightly about this great theme, especially in the light of our current ozone depletion, damage to resources, unbridled technology, and rampant demographic explosion.

Those are all global or international examples which may seem a bit removed from our local context. But we also witness similar problems. Take my own country South Africa as probably typical of many other places around the world.

Urbanisation

In South Africa in 1900, 80 percent of our population lived in rural areas but, by 1996, 80 percent lived in urban areas. This perilous trend will undoubtedly continue. In fact we have one of the highest urbanisation rates in the world with our urban population doubling every fourteen years. Urbanisation of course is also very much a worldwide phenomenon.

Soil erosion

Our nation loses 400 million tons of soil down our rivers every year.

Water scarcity

In Johannesburg, half the household water used is poured onto gardens! Yet South Africa only has enough stored water (given no droughts) to meet our needs for 30 years. Recent reports indicate that in the next two or three decades, southern Africa will be known globally as a region of water scarcity.

Deserts

The Karoo, a semi-desert area in the Northern Cape, seriously affects our nation, since between 1870 and 1970 it spread over an additional 207,000 square kilometres. It is still spreading steadily north and south. Clearly, even on the home front, but also on many others, our environmental problem is pressing.

The world's response

The actions taken by the secular world in dealing with these problems are grounded in an assortment of philosophical postures. I list a few:

Utilitarian

This says we have got to live off the planet and in it, so we'd better not wreck it. This sort of selfish and self-preservationist ecology is not without its value, but by itself it is a shallow base, being purely pragmatic.

Pantheist

Those who have this ecology say one of two things: Either that the human species and nature are all of one essence – i.e., there is no qualitative difference between the human and the natural or animal world or, extending this, they say God is in everything and everything is God. Francis Schaeffer, writing near the beginning of the environmental movement, summed up the pantheistic way of thinking in these terms: "The term 'God's creation' has no real place in pantheistic thinking. One simply does not have a creation, but only an extension of God's essence, in which any such term as 'God's creation' – (as though He were a personal God who created, whose creation was external to himself) ... has no place."[2] One point to note here is that actions based on the idea that "God is in all, and all is part of God" lead to the dehumanising of humanity while elevating nature. Sacred cows can survive in India while humans starve. Moreover, if the cruel, destructive and "red with tooth and claw" parts of nature are all equated with God, then the pantheist is left with a real problem as to the nature of a God who is, in essence, part of all that.

Atheistic

Said Bertrand Russell: "That Man is the product of causes which had no prevision of the end they were achieving; that his origin, his growth, his hopes and fears, his loves and his beliefs, are but the outcome of accidental collocations of atoms; that no fire, no heroism, no intensity of thought and feeling, can preserve an individual life beyond the grave; that all the labours of the ages, all the devotion, all the inspiration, all the noonday brightness of human genius, are destined to extinction in the vast death of the solar system, and that the whole temple of Man's achievement must inevitably be buried beneath the débris of a universe in ruins – all these things, if not quite beyond dispute, are yet so nearly certain, that no philosophy which rejects them can hope to stand. Only within the scaffolding of these truths, only on the firm foundation of unyielding despair, can the soul's habitation henceforth be safely built."[3] Jacques Monod, the molecular biologist, put it this way: "…man knows at last that he is alone in the universe's unfeeling immensity, out of which he has emerged only by chance."[4] Such a posture forbids any really logical concern for anything – social, moral or ecological. Moreover, if the atheist does express such a concern, he runs logically contrary to his own presuppositions. The earth may thus be raped with impunity, for nothing means anything. An even more desperate loss is that of rationality. For, as C.S. Lewis once observed: "If my own mind is the product of the irrational … how shall I trust my mind?"[5]

Religiously apostate

In this posture we know God is there, but we are too distant from Him to care for Him, for others, or for nature. By such rebellion from those who should know better, we see the tragic interconnection between human disobedience and forgetfulness and a host of not only social but environmental problems. Hosea the prophet saw how breaking the covenant with our Creator leads to the rupturing of bonds within the home, within society and between humans and their environment: "...for the Lord has a controversy [lawsuit] with the inhabitants of the land. There is no faithfulness or kindness, and no knowledge of God in the land; there is swearing, lying, killing, stealing, and committing adultery; they break all bounds and murder follows murder. Therefore the land mourns, and all who dwell in it languish, and also the beasts of the field, and the birds of the air; and even the fish of the sea are taken away" (Hosea 4:1-3). The more sinfully humans distance themselves from their God, the more sinfully will they treat and rapaciously rape the environment.

A proper understanding of the environment

What people do regarding the environment and ecology depends on what they think of themselves in relation to the world around them. Our ecological philosophy is controlled by our views of human origins and destiny. We do what we think, as these key points show:

The Christian must start out with a creationist statement

"In the beginning God created the heavens and the earth" (Genesis 1:1). As such, creation is good. It is God's, but it is not a part of God. It has an existence independent of him. He is seen in a tree or a flower, or even an animal – but he is not a tree or a flower or an animal and exists independently. So we are not pantheists ("God is all and all is God"), or Zen Buddhists ("We are all of one essence"), or atheists ("It all comes from impersonal energy, plus time, plus chance") or religious monists ("There is an eternal unity of creator with creation"). "The cosmos is God's body", says one, "an extension of his essence", says another. No! We are biblical and theistic creationists. God created the Natural order but is not part of it.

Indeed, to be at home on Planet Earth requires a worldview that knows from whence Planet Earth came and that it is not our final home. Therefore we neither deify nature in a pantheistic apotheosis and equate it with God, nor do we treat it with less care or importance than it properly deserves as the creation of God. We believe in creation and love it because we first believe in the Creator and love Him! As C.S. Lewis once wrote, "Because we love something else more than this world, we love even this world better than those who know no other."[6] Clearly indeed, if God is involved at all in any part of the physical world, then He is involved everywhere in it. If God is alive and real and active, then all the events of what we call the physical world are dependent on His activity.

Humans are made in the image of God
As such we are qualitatively different from the natural and animal world and vastly more valuable. Jesus never denied the value of sparrows, but he said, "...you are of more value than many sparrows" (Matthew 10:31). So humans are not only more valuable than the natural order, but we have lordship, or "dominion" (Genesis 1:28) over it. We have the power to control it and subdue it but are also to be responsible under God for it.

Thus, while the human beings, as the great "amphibian" between nature and supernature, have an upward relationship to God which gives them meaning, they also have a divinely given downward relationship to nature which gives them responsibility, love and concern for the natural order. They are a guardian and steward of nature and, in the last analysis, they are not dealing with their own possessions, but with God's. They are provisionally in charge, but they are not free to exploit. Our dominion is subsumed under God's dominion.

Created things, being God-created, have an intrinsic value
The tree is entitled to being a tree because God made it. The dog has an intrinsic right to its "dogginess" and to its existence. Everything as part of God's creation is to be treated with the integrity or respect appropriate to its place or level in the created order. Things are not just valuable because they can serve us as humans, but because they are part of God's creation and fit into His overall plan and provision for the planet.

Something has gone wrong in the created order
This is mysterious and is related to our attempt to live independently of God. For the Christian, neither our life as

humans nor the created order we live in is normal. It is abnormal; therefore, there will be things in life, history and nature that are bad, inexplicable, ugly and perplexing. Says Paul: "We know that the whole creation has been groaning in travail together until now" (Romans 8:22). In the preceding verses he states, "For the creation waits with eager longing for the revealing of the sons of God; for the creation was subjected to futility, not of its own will but by the will of him who subjected it in hope; because the creation itself will be set free from its bondage to decay and obtain the glorious liberty of the children of God" (Romans 8:19-21).

Christians therefore believe that the redemption in Christ not only has personal, but cosmic significance. But if we start from pantheistic or monist presuppositions we have real problems because we can have no answer to the fact that nature often behaves malevolently and cruelly. And if God is part of or equated with nature, we have a real problem as to His real nature, for He now becomes part of the imperfect or bad. So Romantic or non-Christian mysticisms at this point leave us with no solution when nature is destructive and negative.

For the biblical Christian, answers lie in accepting the biblical picture of the historic, space-time fall of humankind which had cosmic implications in the natural order, hence God's judgmental curses on the natural order in Genesis 3:14-19. The fact is that, without belief in the historic, space-time fall of humanity, we have other metaphysical and moral problems. For if humans, who are sinful, and nature, which is often cruel, are both part of God and God part of them as per pantheism and monism, then God becomes both sinful and cruel, and His mottled handiwork cannot be challenged, let alone properly stewarded. Baudelaire, the 19th century French poet, saw this and once said, "If there's a God, he is the devil."

But if in fact there is a discontinuity between God and the Created order because free, non-programmed Adamic humanity, created by an infinite, personal and holy God, has changed itself from good to less than good in a space-time rebellion against God as its point of integration and control – a rebellion with cosmic consequences – then we can understand ourselves. We can care, under God, for nature without deifying it, and morals, affecting both human interpersonal behaviour and responsible human ecological responses, can exist. Thus can we not only fight evil and disease in the world without fighting God, but we can fight irresponsible and evil exploitation of nature and the environment, because nature and the environment are finally His and as responsible servants of God we are to have dominion over them.

Although it has been affected by sin, the created order is still there as God's possession and is therefore immensely important and valuable

Christians believe that God has created this external world that is really there, and because He is a reasonable God, we can expect by reason to find order in the universe. And we do. In fact we find more than that. When we study the universe or nature, we know mind is meeting Mind. The whole biblical picture then is of a rational, reasonable and mighty God who as Creator has made heaven and earth and has told us to look after it.

Looking ahead

We should also note that the environmental dilemma is not only about the present but the future. Thus, for the Christian, it is hard to address this theme without also introducing eschatology.

An eschatological hope for history

First, history is not a mad meaninglessness, or a pointless shambles. It is not a road to nowhere, a cul-de-sac, or dead-end. Nor is it absurd, as French existentialists say, "a cosmic farce", or a bad dream.

Rather, history has a key. Christians believe that key is Christ and that all of history converges on Him and diverges from Him. History BC thus explains itself in its movement toward the first coming of Christ, while history AD has its meaning, even if hard for us to discern it now, in its movement toward the climactic consummation of things in the Second Coming of Christ.

German theologian Wolfhart Pannenberg says, "The incarnation of God in Jesus of Nazareth forms the point of reference in relation to which the world's course has its unity and on the basis of which every event and every figure in creation is what it is."[7]

The climactic moments

If this is so, it means that our planet has had two climactic moments in its life and has a third yet to come:

1. Life emerges on a lifeless planet, and history begins.

2. A Nazarene Carpenter rises from the dead on Easter Day, death is conquered, life is affirmed, an eternal dimension is revealed and the universe changes gear.

3. This is the one yet to come. History will be consummated in the triumphant return of Jesus Christ.

Without going into detail about all that the Bible says on this subject, we can at least, as regards the future of planet earth, affirm the following:

4. The world will not go on forever – matter is not eternal. Even science confirms this with its law of entropy and the second law of thermodynamics, i.e., that there is a loss of energy in both the world specifically and the universe generally.

5. Christian eschatology affirms that earth's final destiny lies beyond history and beyond time. And when we remember that God operates supernaturally and in sovereignty over humankind, history, and the physical universe, so we also know that past, present, and future are in His hands.

6. Said Jesus, "All authority in heaven and on earth has been given to me" (Matthew 28:18). Likewise, the course of history and the truths of reality will stand according to the words of Christ. Indeed, His Word will stand when all else, including planet earth, as we know it, has gone. In the middle of His greatest discourse on the consummation of history in Matthew 24, Jesus affirmed: "Heaven and earth will pass away, but my words will not pass away" (verse 35).

Conclusion

All this means that history and our planet are moving to Christ
– for all is His. Says Paul: "He is the image of the invisible God,
the first-born of all creation; for in him all things were created,
in heaven and on earth, visible and invisible, whether thrones
or dominions or principalities or authorities – all things were
created through him and for him. He is before all things, and in
him all things hold together" (Colossians 1:15-17).

Thus, while we may not know exactly what the future holds,
we know who holds the future. Not knowing what will come,
we do know who will come. And when He comes, faith will see
what it has believed and unbelief will have to see what it has
not believed and face the consequences. In the meantime, we
are to steward, guard, and enjoy to the full the Lord's created
order as we know it, until He comes again.

"Even so, come Lord Jesus" (Revelation 22:20 – KJV).

End Notes

1. *Time*, November 1997 special issue, cover.

2. Francis A. Schaeffer, *Pollution and the Death of Man – The Christian View of Ecology* (Wheaton, Illinois: Tyndale House Publishers, 1979), 26.

3. Bertrand Russell, "A Free Man's Worship", 1917, Modern History Sourcebook, Fordham University, <http://www.fordham.edu/halsall/mod/1917russell-worship.html>, March 5, 2006.

4. Jacques Monod, *Chance and Necessity: An essay on the natural philosophy of modern biology* (New York: Alfred A. Knopf, 1971), quoted in Hal's Picks of the Month, Journal of Chemical Education – Chemical Education Resource Shelf, University of Missouri – St. Louis, <http://www.umsl.edu/divisions/artscience/chemistry/books/halspicks/hal2005.html>, March 5, 2006.

5. C.S. Lewis, "The Funeral of a Great Myth", *Christian Reflections* (Grand Rapids, Michigan: William B. Eerdmans Publishing Co., 1967), 89.

6. C.S. Lewis, "Some Thoughts", *God in the Dock: Essays in theology and ethics* (Grand Rapids, Michigan: William B. Eerdmans Publishing Co., 1976), 150.

7. Wolfhart Pannenberg, *Jesus – God and Man* (London: SCM Press Ltd, 1968), 396.